P9-BIK-948

Fight with
- Humored
- Culture strength

p. 19
p. 20
p. 144
p. 147
p. 206

the gay agenda

"Like shooting fish in a barrel, Jack Nichols vanquishes every objection raised by fundamentalist dogma. His book is a useful tool for all those who are resisting the poisonous tide of anti-gay prejudice, ignorance, and fear. Even more helpful is the visionary sensibility imparted along with the practical wisdom."

Mark Thompson, author of *Gay Spirit: Myth and Meaning* and *Gay Soul: Finding the Heart of Gay Spirit and Nature*

the gay agenda

Talking Back to the Fundamentalists

Jack Nichols

With a Foreword by George Weinberg, Ph.D.

 **Prometheus Books**

59 John Glenn Drive
Amherst, NewYork 14228-2197

Published 1996 by Prometheus Books

00 99 98 97 96   5 4 3 2 1

Library of Congress Cataloging-in-Publication Data

Nichols, Jack.
    The gay agenda : talking back to the fundamentalists / Jack Nichols.
        p.   cm.
    Includes bibliographical references and index.
    ISBN 1-57392-103-3 (cloth)
    1. Homosexuality—United States. 2. Religious fundamentalism—United States. 3. Homophobia—Religious aspects—United States.
I. Title.
HQ76.3.U5N52   1996
306.76'6—dc20   96-28085
                                                          CIP

Printed in the United States of America on acid-free paper

To

Steve Yates and Gary Comingdeer

FOR OVER A score of years they have lived and worked together as an inspirer and an artist: male comrades, ever
strong and loving mates. To me they bring laughter, thought,
loyalty, patience, and help extraordinaire. Because of them
the days begin and end easily, happily, and more colorfully. To
thank them for spirited gifts is beyond any reach of my words.
But if words be needed, let it be said that loving kindness lives
passionately in their minds and hearts; that the good, the true
and the beautiful sparkle in their lives; and that I am ever
enriched because of an unfailing, shrewd, and uncanny awareness they bring to each of our endeavors.

Contents

Acknowledgments

To STEVE YATES, for his timely suggestion that I write this book. To Gary Comingdeer, modernist artist in the Cherokee totomistic tradition, for his continuing interest in the project. To my mother, Mary Finlayson Lund, for never-failing friendship. To David Scott Evans for ever-valued appraisals. To Eugene O'Connor and Steven L. Mitchell for expert editorial assistance never before equaled in my career. To Kevin Miller, graphic designer, responsible for this book's handsome dust jacket. To Dr. Franklin Kameny, the father of gay militancy, my comrade-in-arms, early inspirer, and friend. To Barbara Gittings and Kay Tobin Lahusen, pioneering lesbian activists and journalists, a loving couple since 1961 and my longtime friends and comrades in arms. To old friend and gay media pioneer, Randolfe Wicker, who got me my first job in journalism and who keeps me apprised of Manhattan goings-on. To George Ferenz, former *TWN* editor and advisor. To Eric Rhein, innovative New York artist, for inspiring me as he walks boldly with footsteps reminiscent of his extraordinary gay liberationist uncle, my great love, the late Lige Clarke. To

Saviz Shafaie, pioneering Iranian gay and male liberationist. To Bill Wears and Ted Richards, loving comrades for three decades and friends to me even longer. To marriage counselor Susan Forthman and to her husband, William, for continuing friendship. To Mark Tietig, ACLU stalwart, futurist, and legal scholar. To the late Logan Carter who was, for me and many others, the most amazing of the androgynes, an ever-loving presence in my thoughts.

Foreword

*George Weinberg, Ph.D.**

FORTY YEARS AGO, any gay agenda could be at most a dream. In the United States, homosexual men and women were despised, mocked, subjected to physical beatings and even murder. In thirty different states, one could serve five or more years in prison for a single homosexual act with another consenting adult. Not surprisingly, nearly all homosexuals were afflicted with self-hate. If they did not live wholly isolated lives, their meetings were furtive, one-time contacts. The vast majority married, raised families, and felt like freaks of nature.

During the early 1960s, only a very few advocates for gay rights dared meet to discuss their dream of equality and to imagine an agenda. In August 1963, Dr. Franklin E. Kameny, the great pioneering gay activist, mounted, on behalf of the Washington Mattachine Society, a spirited defense against a

---

*Dr. George Weinberg pioneered and publicly championed the concept of "the healthy homosexual." He coined the word "homophobia," which has since become the most acceptable term to describe individual and social animosity toward gay men and lesbians.

11

bill that would outlaw the soliciting of funds for gay causes. At a hearing that ensued on Capitol Hill, Congressman John Dowdy of Texas voiced his paranoia in no uncertain terms.

"Isn't it true that your people have an underground network of over fifty thousand members?"

"We hope to, sir," responded Dr. Kameny coolly.

The dream of such a cadre of supporters was as yet no more realized than the abolitionist's dream of equality was in 1820, or the aspiration that women would get the vote at the start of the twentieth century.

Jack Nichols was one of those early Mattachine members who fought to make the dream of gay rights come true. "The man of action is the true dreamer," wrote Oscar Wilde. I've known Jack and I can attest that he is both a dreamer and a man of action.

Jack had been working for gay rights for many years before the word "gay" entered common parlance. He was active in the fight during the period when even the ACLU refused to accept gay causes. As an assistant to the Washington Bureau Chief of the *New York Post,* he was already honing his skills to articulate important truths. In 1965 Jack was one of about ten gay protesters who dared picket the White House.

True to his dream, Jack has since been joined by many times the fifty thousand advocates that Congressman Dowdy pictured with anticipatory dread. Jack's analyses and proclamations in print have been a great catalyst, not only for gays but for a multitude of human rights advocates.

▼ ▼ ▼

My own experience with gay rights started by chance. During the 1950s, through common interests, I became a close friend of several gay men who shared my love of poetry and literature. We would sit in cafeterias, talking endlessly about the Romantic poets, about Samuel Johnson, and about the salons of eighteenth-century France and England—so-called "faggot stuff."

I valued these friends for their encompassing, loving vision of literature, their gentleness of spirit, their subtlety. At the time, I later came to see, these friends were desperately hiding their homosexuality, even from me. They were notably nonresponsive when I referred to the women I was dating, and now I realize why. Their secrecy about their own lives left me feeling slightly excluded. But my feeling of isolation must have been a thousandth of that terrible sense of isolation and fear which beset them. Only in retrospect can I imagine the self-hate, the dread of retribution, and fear of what even I might say if I found out, which kept them so secretive.

Eventually, a few disclosed to me what they had considered the dark truth of their not being "like others," like me. It was difficult for them to reveal their notion that they did not draw their passions from a common spring. Society, in those days, did not recognize that passion is its own excuse for being and that *all* love is conspiratorial and deviant and magical. The "mainstream" could not accept that isolation is universal, as is every individual's desire to bridge it with love and truth. In this sense we are all the same.

By the time these friends confided in me, I had become a psychotherapist with a Ph.D. in clinical psychology from Columbia. But psychology as taught officially was essentially a vehicle for instilling the most conservative values. Its aim was to make people conform to the most homogenous, controlling standard.

I had been taught to treat homosexuals as if they were inherently sick. and many of my colleagues were so phobic about gays that it even seemed reasonable to torture homosexuals if this would "cure" them. It was hard to enjoy being one of the chosen people, the "heteros," when so many people whom I admired were not invited to the party.

I personally could not be comfortable with the knowledge that Tchaikovsky had spent a tortured life because he was homosexual and had finally committed suicide for that reason. I felt terrible for Shakespeare, my hero, when, in a sonnet, the poet begged an unnamed lover not to mourn for him too openly after he died:

> Lest the wide world should look into your moan
> And mock you with me after I am gone.

Clearly, Shakespeare was speaking to a gay lover. No one would have mocked a woman for mourning a man. I was outraged that even the greatest of all writers had lived in fear because of his unpopular preference. Love is love, after all, psychoanalysis notwithstanding.

Tormented by the injustice toward gays, I began speaking out publicly and soon identified the syndrome which I named "homophobia." I used the term deliberately because the reaction to gays was clearly phobic. As time when on, I became what was then called a "homophile," and eventually was introduced to those in the vanguard of the incipient gay movement.

The moment I met Jack Nichols, I realized that not only did we view existence similarly but that we had the same dreams for the future. We shared a humanist agenda. Jack's gay agenda no more required that I become homosexual than my agenda required that he give it up. Quite the contrary, we both believed that sexual and romantic fulfillment, in whatever form moves you. offers the highest likelihood of living humanely and creatively with others.

I was delighted when, in 1969, Jack founded and became

co-editor of the newspaper *Gay*, the first weekly newspaper for gay people distributed on newsstands. My discussions with Jack led to a series of articles in *Gay*, in which I examined my concept of homophobia from many angles, discussing the syndrome, its origins, its effects on the personality of the homophobe, its implications for society, and its cures. It was wonderful to write for Jack, who was wise and cultured and fair, and who introduced me to some of the brightest activists in the country. My articles in *Gay* led me to write a book describing homophobia. The term caught on, and more people were alerted to its dangers.

Jack's newspaper and his prolific, impassioned writings elsewhere brought tens of thousands out of the closet. He gave people faith in themselves, faith in what a society could be at its best, and faith in love. Not so different from the essential messages of Jesus, who himself never explicitly condemned homosexuality and who always championed empathy and sided with the oppressed.

Since about 1970, the number of openly gay people and activists has been multiplying fast. Jack and his little band of dreamers now have plenty of company. Homophobia is today a common word. This year it entered the stuffy though superb *Oxford English Dictionary*, but Jack's newspaper spread the word first.

Jack Nichols has always been more interested in bringing people into the movement than in aggrandizing himself. Now that he stands arm in arm with a multitude, many newcomers may not realize that for a long time he stood alone. His receiving less than full credit doesn't matter to Jack, but it does to me. I think that Jack, like the other early activists, ought to get much more credit than they do for crusading at a dangerous time. The threat to gay activists was real, as evidenced by the murder of Lige Clarke, Jack's lover and activist partner.

Jack has gone on to speak and to write books and newspaper columns advancing humanist causes. But his writings are more than polemics and his true subject matter is always broader than the topics he addresses.

In this book, *The Gay Agenda,* he again goes far beyond his ostensible scope, which is the danger of fundamentalism taken to extremes. As Jack sees it, fundamentalism is a movement that purports to take the Bible as its sole authority and to take the words of the Bible literally. But, as Jack points out, fundamentalists tend to use the Bible selectively for their purposes, citing the Old Testament in condemning homosexuals but neglecting to add that those who work on the Sabbath are also seen to be in the wrong.

As always, Jack is examining a bigger subject than the local one he writes about. He brings to bear a world of references from the past and present to make his case, which is a deeply spiritual one. His battle is for acceptance of all people despite their differences. It is against hate campaigns and for what he calls "the maximization of affection." Jack Nichols foresees a world in which narrow and exclusive interpretations of lovemaking give way to a deeper appreciation of real human differences.

He is writing not just about fundamentalism but about humanism, not just about gays but about people. He is writing as much for religious people as for nonreligious ones. I have always thought that the real message of homosexuality holds for all of us, no matter how dissimilar we seem to be. This message. embodied in *The Gay Agenda,* is an inalienable truth, that the surface differences between people are less important than our need to care for one another. This truth I teamed more from Jack Nichols than from any other person.

Democracy and the
Gay, Lesbian, and Bisexual Movements

For you these from me, O Democracy, to serve you ma femme!
For you, for you I am trilling these songs.

Walt Whitman[1]

*T*HE "GAY AGENDA" is a term that has been coined for propaganda purposes by the forces of religious fundamentalism. To enhance what they would have others believe is the
ominous dimension of this term, they also refer to "the homosexual agenda." Morality police manipulate religious taboos
against a natural and age-old sexual variation, stirring fears
about the imaginary growth of a latter-day Sodom and Gomorrah, which, by the way, is an effective fund-raising technique.
Same-sex love is advertised by opportunistic scriptural selec-
tivists as, perhaps, "the worst moral calamity that can befall an
individual or a civilization."

While same-sex relationships are as old as history, the word
"homosexual" originated only in the last century, while "gay"
has emerged only in the past few decades among both men
and women as a word suitable for in-group identification and

which is now gaining in popular usage. Among the orthodox, prior to the arrival of these words, same sex-contact was considered only a kind of aberrant behavior. This mistaken view was possible because sex, without reference to affection, was highlighted. Emotional contact between same-sex couples remained, except between the couple concerned, an unknown. The taboo against same-sex passion allowed labels like "pervert," "deviate," and "degenerate," implying that gay men and lesbians were merely wayward or oversexed heterosexuals in search of perverse thrills. The ensuing gay and lesbian social revolution evolved in response to this error, requiring an impartial term that would allow the neutrality needed for affirmative self-identities. This new term—"gay"—stood for both the person and for his or her experience of same-sex affection, molding, in the process, a major stepping stone of social change. Lighthearted, yet so ordinary as not to arouse hostile suspicions, "gay" became usable as both adjective and noun. The word "lesbian," for several decades, was regarded by some to be a pejorative term. Later, though many same-sex-oriented women continued to refer to themselves as "gay," most began, after the 1970s, to refer to themselves pridefully as "lesbians," thereby reclaiming a word with ancient origins. Sappho, who lived on the island of Lesbos in the Aegean Sea, loved women. She was antiquity's greatest poetess.

Religious fundamentalists, however, as a matter of strategy, still define homosexuality in terms of sex acts alone. We who are gay-identified reject this approach, knowing that all-around affection is, as among opposite-sex lovers, the major focus of our self-definition. Through desire and experience grow the primary roots of our relationships which reach beyond the confines of the sex act. But because we have been denied our humanity due to the deliberate fundamentalist focus on sex, there has risen a desperate need for self-reclamation. The first scientific survey of sexual behavior in America, popularly known as The Kinsey Report, took place in 1948.[2] Dr. Alfred Kinsey's nonjudgmental continuum between heterosexuality and homosexuality demonstrates that there can be integration of affection irrespective of gender. Because of the anti-sexual fundamentalist emphasis, the movement for gay and lesbian equality arose. Fundamentalist culture can thus credit itself, because of its bigotry, for making necessary the very liberation movement it now so vocally opposes. /В

In the last half of the nineteenth century, when human affectional relations first interested theoretical researchers like Richard von Krafft-Ebing, it seemed possible, without fear of contradiction, to lump together various sexual manifestations, some of them abusive. Pedophiles, for example, were thought by some to be exclusively same-sex oriented. Following up on this, today's hate-stirring fundamentalist preachers celebrate serial murderers John Gacy and Jeffrey Dahmer as representative of gays generally. Careful students of sexuality know, however, that antisocial acts occur most frequently among males conditioned or attracted to the opposite sex. Even so, at either end of the sexual continuum—gay or straight—sex-violent behavior is clearly nurtured by the more pervasive culture of repression and strict sexual silence /В favored by fundamentalists. This suppressed force, having no link to the fact of sexual orientation itself, has, like a viper, been secretly curled within this suppression they promote. Ignorance of sexual matters and the shame cast by society over healthy sexual expression, leads the ignorant to commit rape and other forms of coercion. Just as opposite-sexers have no reason to self-identify with serial murderers Ted Bundy or Richard Speck, so do same-sexers not self-identify with Gacy and Dahmer. In recent years it has become obvious that the overwhelming majority of sexually criminal acts, including incest, child molestation, and rape, are committed by those identified as being within the sexual majority. When sexually criminal acts are perpetrated by gays, they seem to occur most often among closeted types who preach anti-gay doctrines, as evidenced by the avalanche of charges of sexual abuse of minors launched in recent years against "celibate" Catholic priests. "Some analysts," says Reverend Enda McDonagh, an Irish theologian who is President of the National Conference of Priests, "feel the scandal will weaken the church's authority."[3] By contrast, sexual violence among those openly gay is so rare as to be almost nonexistent.

Even cursory observation reveals that gay-identified men and lesbians are individually as various and unique as Americans everywhere, emerging from every walk of life, espousing differing philosophies and religions, and as sexually constrictive or expansive as the sexual majority itself. Many gay men and lesbians are as easily influenced by cultural fads as are their non-gay friends and neighbors. Within the amorphous bounds of gay communities are men and women both rich and poor, people of undoubted genius as well as the most abjectly ignorant. They surely sustain Abraham Lincoln's observation that: "God must have loved the common people because he made so many of them." At Cherry Grove, for example, one of Fire Island's gay summer resorts, one can watch middle-aged and elderly same-sex Texas couples play canasta in the afternoon or, in the evening, attend theatrical productions where admission fees raise funds for community upkeep. Ecology, a constant concern of Cherry Grove homeowners, takes precedence, in public forums, over all other discussions. Sex, as elsewhere, is a matter of private concern.

▼ ▼ ▼

Between 1940 and 1970 there stood, in the nation's capital, a gay bar three blocks from the White House. There a pianist held court till closing time, playing golden oldies and the latest hits. On weekends, in the mid–1950s, this friendly bar was filled to the rafters with people reflecting life's kaleidoscope: some looking nervously about at the frolicking multitudes, others wanting nothing more than a cold beer, and a few hoping desperately to meet Mister Right. The pianist played a local theme song, a holdover, perhaps, from World War II when uniformed youths, hoping for a last fling before they shipped out to foreign battlefields, sang along. Its lyrics celebrated the company of a pharmacist's mate, known today as naval corpsman:

> *I don't want to get well,*
> *I don't want to get well,*
> *I'm in love with a pharmacist's mate.*
> *Early in the morning, night and noon,*
> *A great big handsome sailor comes and feeds me*
> *   with a spoon. . . .*

The bar had the atmosphere of a college hangout, and in the days before gay liberation was in full swing, one could sit and watch the faces of young and old, as yet unsure of the propriety of their orientations, singing gaily as the pianist lit up this little bar with poignant strains. Beer mugs were lifted high. Smiles and frowns, confidence and uncertainty: those who were handsome, and those not so fortunate, seemed during such moments to be bound in a spirited brotherhood extending far beyond the confines of the bar to similar locales throughout the length and breadth of America; thousands of harmless rendezvous points, hardly the dens of iniquity hysterically envisioned by puritans.

One unmistakable trait, observable elsewhere after the

mid–1950s, was the growth of an enhanced democracy in action within America's gay subcultures. Every race, religion, and class began, in certain locales, to mingle. This highlighted more than the diversity of the gay subcultures. It also showed that people, discriminated against on account of race, gender, or sexual preference, seek solidarity-bolstering self-esteem in the face of irrational condemnation.

Edward Sagarin, a sociologist who, under the pseudonym "Donald Webster Cory," penned, in 1951, the gay equivalent of Betty Friedan's *The Feminine Mystique,* wrote:

> The homosexual, cutting across all racial, religious, national, and caste lines, frequently reacts to rejection by a deep understanding of all others who have likewise been scorned because of belonging to an outcast group. . . . The person who has felt the sting of repudiation by the dominant culture can reflect that, after all, he might have been of another religion or race or color, an untouchable in India, one of the mentally or physically handicapped. It is not for him to join in with those who reject millions of their fellow men of all types and groups, but to accept all men, an attitude forced upon him happily by the stigma of being cast out of the fold of society.[4]

History chronicles such democratic camaraderie in the last century, affecting even such class-conscious societies as Great Britain's. It has been noted that Oscar Wilde (1854–1900) had confessed, when accused of "posing as a Sodomite," to associating with men beneath his station. His countrymen saw such associations not as democratic strengths, however, but as unwelcome weaknesses, suggestive themselves, in fact, of homosexual inclinations.

The American poet Walt Whitman (1819–1892) was criticized for celebrating "adhesive" emotional relationships among those of the same sex, no matter their class, race, age, or religion He foresaw, in fact, "a continent made indissoluble" through the "manly love of comrades." Whitman's long-time companion, Peter Doyle, was a streetcar conductor. The English writer Edward Carpenter (1844–1929), author of the poetic work *Towards Democracy,*[5] took to his aristocratic side a commoner, a rural workman, George Merrill, and moved from the judgmental environs of London, where he'd found social life stilted and suffocating, to orchards near the Scottish border town of Sheffield. There, these two men lived happily, doing manual labor while Carpenter wrote books. Their home was open to other great thinkers of the time.

In spite of such democratic leanings, the gay subcultures have produced, in both past and present times, famous individualists whose fundamental approaches to life differ radically from the majority. There is no more solidarity of opinion among those attracted to their own sex than among those who prefer opposites. Sexual orientation is no guarantor of one's political or philosophical approach. Since gay people come from every corner of the political and social spectrum, uncloseted figures like Paul Goodman, the neo-anarchist philosopher, could have hypothetically unwittingly brushed elbows with a closeted self-hating nemesis like McCarthyite Roy Cohn. Both men were gay. Both shared Jewish roots. An examination of their life histories, however, proves that their political agendas burned brightly in wholly divergent arenas. Goodman's published diaries, titled *Five Years,* chronicle a lackluster period during the 1950s, explaining without shame how he sought the affectional company of males. Legal expert Roy Cohn, working as Senator Joseph McCarthy's foremost counsel, hid his "shameful" same-sex feelings, adding to a grim period unsurpassed for hypocritical political witch-hunts, pointing fingers of scorn, hoping to rid the State Department of its "homos" and "perverts."

▼　▼　▼

Famed gay authors, artists, actors, academics, politicians, warriors, composers, athletes, and clergy provide a no-nonsense introduction to the undeniable fact that on any issue, individual variation among them is as great as that in the world at large. Even within the most prestigious confines of conservative bastions there are men and women whose homosexual leanings have been publicized. Former Maryland Congressman Robert Bauman, Republican author of *The Conscience of a Gay Conservative,*[6] was, before being forced from his closet, a major opponent of gay liberation gains. Uncloseted Congressman Barney Frank, the liberal Democrat from Massachusetts, openly gives unabashed support to gay rights. Stage and screen stars like Liberace and Rock Hudson hid the fact that they were gay-identified, a fact which became widely known only after they died of AIDS. Popular singers like Elton John and k.d. lang have stated that they are gay, thus avoiding those discomforts caused by a closet lifestyle.

Jean Genet, a petty thief and longtime prisoner, as well as a great novelist and playwright, celebrated his homosexuality as a form of anti-social action, while the philosopher Plato wrote of same-sex liaisons as a necessary cement for the social order. These views are so antithetical that even a casual perusal of either's approach reveals the distance between their perspectives. To stereotype and lump together gay men and lesbians, as the fundamentalists do, shows only willful ignorance. The rich variety so clearly a hallmark on the homosexual side of the human continuum remains unnoticed most by those who refuse to look. The strict, serious moralism of

André Gide or the laughing, satirical laxity of Oscar Wilde demonstrates how two gay contemporaries can arrive on the field of ideas from totally opposite poles. Erte painted frivolous art deco fantasy women, while the sadomasochistic photographer Robert Mapplethorpe focused on the heavy leather underside of Manhattan night life. Academic Camille Paglia, a lesbian and the author of *Sexual Personae* as well as a darling of conservative talk show hosts, critiques popular writer Rita Mae Brown for supposed "tunnel vision, lack of hard political knowledge, indifference to aesthetics and shrill reductiveness" in her book *Sex, Art and American Culture* (p. 112).

Harry Hay, the West Coast founder of the original Mattachine Society, and thus a seminal character in the American gay movement, later founded also a rural, nationwide group popularly known as The Radical Faeries. Hay has little in common with Dr. Franklin E. Kameny, the East Coast strategist who has worked tirelessly, as the undisputed father of gay militancy, to secure employment rights for gays in government, including entrance to the military. The Radical Faeries, whose fashions still reflect the long-hairs of the sixties counterculture, are more likely to ridicule established government orthodoxy and would be the least likely of groups to crusade for the rights of gay men and lesbians to don military uniforms. Fairy gatherings, held mostly in natural settings, find attendees seated in friendly circles reminiscent of Native American groupings. They share thoughts and, afterwards, enjoy performing rituals common in pagan or erstwhile New Age spiritual assemblages. Dr. Kameny, on the other hand, has used Robert's Rules of Order to guide the major democratic liberation organizations he has inspired, and, being a Harvard-trained astronomer, Kameny the scientist waxes openly hostile to occultism or mysticism, being particularly intolerant of the "science" of astrology.

▼ ▼ ▼

In 1965 there were barely twenty "gay" organizations in the United States, most of them one-person operations, though a few, in major cities such as Washington, D.C., boasted as many as a hundred brave members. In 1966 the first national meeting of gay and lesbian organizations convened in Kansas City. Only eight metropolitan areas were represented. Not until the late sixties and the eruption of the Stonewall rebellion (a foiled police raid on a Greenwich Village gay bar), did the gay and lesbian liberation movement mushroom, jumping from a mere forty organizations in 1969 to four hundred in 1973. Today there are at least five thousand groups nationwide, but each, like the varied sections of the nation they represent, remains unique and individualistic, geared to the needs of gay men and lesbians in disparate and varied locales.

Within today's gay subcultures are organizations touching every corner of the ideological spectrum. The Universal Fellowship of Metropolitan Community Churches (MCC), founded in 1968 by the Reverend Troy Perry, an openly gay minister, is a rapidly growing Christian denomination, which fills a gap, as black churches do, for segregated parishioners. The "Christian" majority is relieved thereby of having to brush elbows with openly gay men and lesbians who consider themselves Christians but who experience an outpouring of judgmentalism mixing in traditional Christian environs. MCC churches combine Episcopal ritual with a fiery Baptist preaching style, attracting members from various points on the denominational scale. If it were not for the fact that same-sex couples fill MCC pews, it would be difficult to point to major differences between these gay-friendly churches and mainstream sects. The Reverend Perry preaches that a love of self, a love of God, and a love for America are paramount. He believes, however, that the homosexual has to love himself before anybody else can love him, and that "anybody," he says, includes God. One must come to terms with oneself, says Perry, knowing what one is and knowing what one wants out of life.

Major denominations must deal with gay believers who choose to remain within the mainstream, working to change the anti-gay views of their hierarchies. The Roman Catholic group is called *Dignity* and the Episcopalian group, *Integrity*. Gay Jews have, in several major cities, established their own synagogues. Gay Mormans and Christian Scientists support organizations hoping to change the intractable anti-gay dogmas their faiths promote. At the opposite pole has stood a recently collapsed organization of American Gay and Lesbian Atheists; New York author and gay witch, Dr. Leo Louis Martello, writes occult books and practices his Wiccan faith, The Old Religion. Native American shamans, often homosexually inclined, assured a place for those like themselves in tribal cultures while the celebrated author Christopher Isherwood introduced his readers to Indian mystics from the Asian subcontinent.

Dividing points in America's gay communities have, since the onset of the liberation movement, often surfaced in discussions between men and women. As in the general population, lifestyles often differ. The law, which has seldom dealt with lesbianism or, in fact, recognized its existence, affects gay men differently. Like their straight-male counterparts some gay men have, while keeping their orientations secret, generally enjoyed employment opportunities unknown to lesbians because they are women. The relevance of feminist issues, therefore, often escapes these men. Lesbians, nevertheless, have joined gay men to battle AIDS, often with great compassion and courage. Their equal presence at great gay and lesbian marches in Washington, D.C., New York, and elsewhere, has heartened both men and women to whom such marches seem to effectively highlight their own high stakes in the ongoing struggle for same-sex lovers' liberation.

Variety in such marches, as everywhere in affectionate same sex environs, is evident. There are gay and bisexual integrationists and gay isolationists, comprising those who would mingle with denizens of the world at large, and those who say they feel most comfortable in segregated gay ghettos. There are gay assimilationists, eager to take their part in the establishment, and there are homosexual anarchists who would undermine values supporting what they consider the establishment's rotting culture. The vast majority of gay men and lesbians, however, take little interest in such distinctions. Like other Americans, they simply go to work, visit friends, and tend to domestic chores.

Unless touched by discrimination, only a minority of gay men and lesbians are likely to join gay organizations. There are those that cater to both gay Democrats and gay Republicans. There is a rapidly growing alternative youth culture, with its own music, dance, and mostly opposite-sex orientation, but in which same-sex lovers are comfortably integrated in many inner city nightclubs. There are national organizations such as Black and White Gay Men Together, an organization promoting same-sex racial integration. There are gay health maintenance groups, gay gyms, gay societies for the hearing-impaired, gay bingo games, gay bowling leagues, gay dart clubs, gay business associations, and gay ethnic celebrations. Ethnic differences add to gay cultural variety just as they do in straight communities. The Gay Games, an international competition, has attracted athletes from nearly fifty countries. Gay rodeos, held mostly in Western states, demonstrate beyond a shadow of a doubt how varied are the interests of ordinary people who have only their sexual orientations in common.

While the concept of equal rights for American citizens has become a constant in the consciousness of these participants, there is little else about their views that can be called monolithic. Within the nation's gay and lesbian community, just as in the pluralistic America where it thrives, there is a vast mix of individuals long accustomed to deciding their personal agendas. But there has never been much likelihood for a completely unified outlook that could fit, with any degree of accuracy, the fundamentalists' claim that there is a malicious or secret gay agenda, one that works to undermine society and is accepted by all gay men and lesbians. Could there be such gay unanimity? Hardly. Writing in 1973, New York Mattachine pioneer Dick Leitsch said: "The gay world is the oldest permanently floating anarchy on earth."[7]

▼ ▼ ▼

Most gay, lesbian, and bisexual Americans might agree perhaps that law-abiding adults, differing in their tastes from the majority, eschewing coercion and embracing mutual consent, deserve both bedroom privacy and, in matters outside the bedroom, treatment no different from their fellows. Fundamentalist propagandists, in their zeal to control the affectional lives of ordinary citizens, pretend that "the gay agenda" demands "special rights," such as the "right" to molest children or to beg taxes for the financing of transsexual operations. They have organized nationally and internationally to denounce same-sex love, using shameless lies to erect every conceivable stumbling block they can put in its path. But we who stand for the equal right of such love to exist beg no inflammatory "special rights," as these fundamentalist proselytizers claim, but only simple fair play to assure we are not deprived, by these tireless, interfering "religious" fanatics, of equal employment security, housing, and access to the kind of general safety enjoyed by our fellow citizens. If there is no coherent "gay agenda," no nationwide gay plan, is there, in fact, a specific agenda that deals with homosexuality? *Yes*, but not one produced by gays; rather, it is created by anti-gay fundamentalists who would gladly reinstate the death penalty prescribed in the Book of Leviticus for same-sex couples. Conveniently forgetting other odd biblical commands such as that in Leviticus 23:30, which demands the death penalty for those who work on the Sabbath, religious fundamentalists have discovered that same-sex hate mongering gets them the most mileage, enabling them, as did Joseph Goebbels, minister of propaganda in Hitler's Germany, to point at recognizable people and, with vicious lies, to stir up animosity against them.

Nineteenth-century religionists were able to crusade against masturbators, whom they called onanists, and their tabooed practice, onanism. Fictions were spread about the growth of hair on onanists' palms, of their going insane or losing otherwise healthy complexions.[8] In retrospect, it would seem that this taboo was a Middle Eastern tribe's attempt to keep its population growing. A "religious" crusade against masturbators today, however, would backfire, especially since masturbation is the most universal sexual practice.

Religious fundamentalists pick and choose which biblical taboos to enforce. In the Bible, as others note, there are only six specific statements relating to same-sex lovemaking. The most famous and inflammatory of these (which includes a death penalty and which is cited regularly by fundamentalist televangelists to publicly justify the killing of gay males) is Leviticus 20:13, written centuries before the birth of Jesus (who, incidentally, had nothing to say on such matters). No such punishment is found in the Bible for lesbian behavior. The "religious" incitors to gay male murders, however, ignore other biblical citations, such as that which requires any prostitute daughter of a religious leader to be burned alive (Lev. 21:9), or that children (or adults) who curse their parents must die (Lev. 20:9), or that males having sex with their wives while she is having her period must be "cut off from among their people" (Lev. 20:18). But, like Hitler's propaganda minister, fundamentalist preachers sway a large and often ignorant constituency that will vent their frustrations and dissatisfactions on scapegoated others. The inflammatory and false agenda they thus create, and the evil purpose it serves, is to deprive "other" citizens not only of their right to make love, but of their homes and, indeed, the very jobs through which they support and feed themselves. While most Americans, upon hearing the word "fundamentalist," would associate it with biblical literalists, television preachers, or ranting evangelicals, the label "fundamentalism" may also be applied to any group marked by a rigid adherence to given dogma. Whether a pope propelled by a belief in his own infallibility or anybody motivated by an inflexible interpretation of "divinely revealed" scriptures, fundamentalists perpetually pursue their own agenda, meddling in the lives of whoever does not share their beliefs.

One reads contemptuously of bearded Islamic fundamentalists running amok in Egyptian, Iranian, and Algerian cities, hoping to catch women who show too much hair or who have allowed forbidden glimpses of their faces, ankles, or arms. These fanatics, out to trash censored books and films, are busily creating theological dictatorships. Their American "Christian" counterparts look to a day when they will wield similar power. The Reverend Jerry Falwell insists that while Khomeini's Iran remains a theocracy, "a Moslem state," he, Falwell, offers "something ten million worlds better, a Judaeo-Christian state."[9] Smug fundamentalists like Falwell whispered sweet nothings in presidential ears during the Reagan-Bush years; but today, under Ralph Reed and his mentor, Pat Robertson, the threat of a fundamentalist politicizing of America has become a living fact. Robert Boston, who works in the Washington, D.C., offices of Americans and Others United For the Separation of Church and State, has penned a frightening and damning portrait of Robertson's agenda.[10] Its death-dealing influences, not only on the lives of American gay males, lesbians, and bisexuals, but on all citizens, will continue, no doubt, well into the next century.

Is it true, as insinuated and taught by fundamentalists that the founding fathers of the United States built the American nation upon the particular doctrines that they preach? Let us see.

NOTES

1. Walt Whitman, "For You O Democracy," *Leaves of Grass* (Amherst, N.Y.: Prometheus Books, 1995), p. 99.

2. Alfred C. Kinsey, Wardell B. Pomeroy, and Clyde E. Martin, *Sexual Behavior in the Human Male* (Philadelphia: W. B. Saunders. 1948); also Wardell B. Pomeroy, Clyde E. Martin, and Paul H. Gebhard, "Concepts of Normality and Abnormality in Sexual Behavior," in Paul Hoch and Joseph Zubin, eds., *Psychosexual Development in Health and Disease* (New York: Grune and Stratton, 1949), pp. 11–32.

3. James F. Clarity, "Catholic Church in Ireland Faces Sex Abuse Scandals," *New York Times*, October 19, 1995, p. A–7. Also Gene Yasuda and Jim Leusner, "Diocese Busy Paying for Sins of Its Fathers: with another pedophilia lawsuit just settled, and others pending, the local diocese continues to find itself mired in controversy over sexual offenses by priests," *Orlando Sentinel*, September 17, 1995, p. 1.

4. Donald Webster Cory, *The Homosexual in America* (New York: Greenberg, 1951), pp. 151–52.

5. Edward Carpenter (1944–1927), *Towards Democracy* (London, T. Fisher Unwin, 1892).

6. Joann Stevens, "The Boy Whore World," *Washington Post,* October 7, 1980, p. 1.

7. Dick Leitsch, "Gay Lore's Heroes and Bores," *GAY,* August 1973.

8. See Vern L. Bullough and Bonnie Bullough, *Sexual Attitudes: Myths and Realities* (Amherst, N.Y.: Prometheus Books, 1995), pp. 73–76.

9. Jerry Falwell in *Thy Kingdom Come,* a film by Antony Thomas, 1988.

10. Robert Boston, *The Most Dangerous Man in America? Pat Robertson and the Rise of the Christian Coalition* (Amherst, N.Y.: Prometheus Books, 1996).

Reason, Unitarian, Deist
Paine
Jefferson
Franklin

A Critique of Fundamentalist Dogmas

My own mind is my own church.
                              Thomas Paine[1]

RELIGIOUS FUNDAMENTALISTS REMIND listeners *ad nauseam* that the United States was founded upon Christian principles, implying that their dogmas—which fuel homophobia as well as other phobias—helped create this nation. In doing so they ignore the flight from Europe of Dutch Reform and Plymouth Brethren immigrants fleeing religious tyranny, especially that of the Puritans, as well as the founding fathers' distrust of majority Christian opinion. Today's homophobia is not only being deliberately fueled by fundamentalist dogmatism, but there are certain orthodox Christian beliefs, especially the doctrine of Original Sin, that subvert social harmony and self-esteem among homosexuals and heterosexuals alike.

When the Puritans arrived on American shores, they set about enforcing their own agenda, crushing dissent with accusations of witchcraft, a ploy not unlike that used by fundamentalists against gay men and lesbians today. The word "fag-

NB

got" has its origins in the penalties of death these "Christians" enforced, faggots being the dry sticks they piled at the base of stakes on which dissenters were burned alive.

The original Plymouth colony settlers were Congregation-alists, forerunners of the modern-day Unitarian Universalist movement. Their communal arrangements were, by present-day standards, socialistic, with all members working and enjoy-ing an equal share of the goods produced. Members of the Society of Friends, or Quakers, were also among the earliest settlers. Their doctrine pointed toward an immanent deity, an inner light, as opposed to majority Christian opinion which looked outward and beyond the skies to an external God. This doctrine of immanence, refusing the ministrations of clergy as intermediaries, helped fashion an individualism in early American culture. Quaker community members would speak their own minds rather than listen to ministers, connecting, they felt, with the inner light. In 1963 a group of British Quak-ers produced a pamphlet titled *Toward a Quaker View of Sex.*[2] This pioneering statement discovered equal value in homo-sexual relationships provided they were imbued with loving care. As our gay, lesbian, and bisexual liberation movement emerged, it was Unitarian/Universalist ministers and Quaker spokespersons who argued first among religionists in support of our civil rights.

The earliest Baptists, unlike the Southern Baptists today, staunchly supported the separation of church and state, know-ing from experience the pain and tyranny resulting from state-supported religion. Presbyterians, also firm supporters of reli-gious freedoms, were nevertheless criticized for their Calvinist underpinnings by the principal strategists who molded the American revolution.

▼ ▼ ▼

The American founding fathers showed that their own fears of religious tyranny were manifold. Thomas Paine, credited with having inspired the American Revolution, wrote *Age of Reason* in the hope that the successful political revolt he had helped engineer would be best followed by a revolution against religious orthodoxy. He wrote:

> I do not believe in the creed professed by the Jewish Church, by the Roman Church, by the Greek Church, by the Turkish Church, by the Protestant Church, nor by any church that I know of. My own mind is my own church. . . . All national institutions of churches, whether Jewish, Christian or Turkish, appear to me no other than human inventions, set up to terrify and enslave mankind, and monopolize power and profit.[3]

Paine's publisher was indicted for blasphemy and imprisoned. Orthodox believers hanged Paine in effigy. While helping revolutionaries in France, he was thrown in jail to await execution, and not even President George Washington, a faithful Episcopalian, answered his letters or spoke on his behalf. Following his critiques of religion Paine became, because of "Christian" influences, persona non grata, and is even now seldom accorded his rightful preeminent place in American history. It is reported that "Christians" dug up his bones so that no one would know where he's buried. It may have been for the best, believe his admirers, because Thomas Paine had called himself "a citizen of the world."

Paine's *Age of Reason* converted many to deism, a belief in God without any divinely inspired spokespersons or books. Other founding fathers had shared this faith, which seems apropos, inasmuch as they had been witness to the ills caused by the competing followers of established creeds. They hoped to protect a new country from the aggressive impulses unleashed by "religious" crusades. If Washington was afraid to be seen publicly with Paine, Jefferson, who was also a deist, was not. He walked the streets arm in arm with Paine after the latter's return from France. Jefferson's autobiography tells how the clauses in the Constitution establishing religious freedom met with fierce opposition, but, he says, the preamble declared that its protection of opinion was meant to be total. Jefferson writes that when it was agreed that "coercion is a departure from the plan of the holy author of our religion," an amendment was proposed to insert the words "Jesus Christ," so that it read "a departure from the plan of Jesus Christ, the holy author of our religion." This proposed insertion, Jefferson exults, was rejected by "a great majority." He then reflects that this was "proof that they meant to comprehend, within the mantle of its protection, the Jew and the Gentile, the Christian and Mahometan, the Hindoo, and Infidel of every denomination."[4]

In 1787 Jefferson advised Peter Carr on how to approach religion in the following words: "Fix reason firmly in her seat, and call to her tribunal every fact, every opinion. Question with boldness even the existence of God; because if there be one, He must more approve of the homage of reason, than that of blindfolded fear. You will naturally examine first the religion of your own country. Read the Bible, then, as you would Livy or Tacitus."[5]

Jefferson didn't trust the clergy. "The clause of the Constitution," he wrote,

> which, while it secured the freedom of the press, covered also the freedom of religion, had given to the clergy a very favorable hope of obtaining an establishment of a particular form of Christianity through the United States; and as every

sect believes its own form the true one, every one perhaps hoped for his own. The returning good sense of our country threatens abortion to their hopes, and they believe that any portion of power confided to me, will be exerted in opposition to their schemes. And they believe rightly: for I have sworn upon the altar of God, eternal hostility against every form of tyranny over the mind of man. But this is all they have to fear from me: and enough too in their opinion.

The doctrine of Christ's divinity was not palatable to Jefferson nor was that concerning Christ's immaculate conception, his creation of the world, his miraculous powers, and his resurrection and visible ascension. Jefferson rejected the idea that Jesus' corporeal body is present in the Eucharist, as well as the Trinitarian concept of God and harmful doctrines like those of the atonement and original sin. These he clearly referred to as "artificial systems" invented by ultra-"Christian" sects unauthorized by a single word spoken by Jesus, and unnecessary as stepping stone beliefs promoting the good life. The very human Jesus admired by Jefferson experienced, he writes,

> the ordinary fate of those who attempt to enlighten and reform mankind, [and] fell an early victim to the jealousy and combination of the altar and the throne, at about thirty-three years of age, his reason having not yet attained the maximum of its energy, nor the course of his preaching, which was but of three years at most, presented occasions for developing a complete system of morals. . . . Hence the doctrines which he really delivered were defective as a whole, and fragments only of what he did deliver have come to us mutilated, misstated, and often unintelligible.

Jefferson spoke forcefully against the idea of divine revelation, thus removing himself entirely from the fundamentalist

Christian purview and making of himself a deistic Unitarian, a religion he said he expected to overtake others. "I confidently expect that the present generation will see Unitarianism become the general religion of the United States," he prophesied. Jefferson, like Benjamin Franklin, preached situation ethics. "Utility," he wrote, "is the test of virtue."

Benjamin Franklin, writing about toleration, explained how it is possible to "look back into history for the character of present sects in Christianity." There he found "Christian" persecutors and Christians who complained they were being persecuted by "Christians" and others. The primitive Christians, Franklin said, "thought persecution extremely wrong in Pagans but practiced it on one another." The first Protestants of the Church of England, "blamed persecution in the Roman Church, but practiced it against the Puritans: these found it wrong in the Bishops, but fell into the same practice themselves both here and in New England." Franklin would thus have quickly flunked fundamentalist litmus tests. His descriptions of closed-mindedness hits them too near home:

> I imagine a man must have a good deal of Vanity who believes, and a good deal of Boldness who affirms, that all the doctrines he holds are true; and all he rejects are false. And perhaps the same may be said of every Sect, Church and Society of men when they assume to themselves that infallibility which they deny to the Popes and Councils. I think Opinions should be judged of by their Influences and Effects."[6]

Was this founding father a Christian? Not by fundamentalist standards. While Franklin thought Jesus to have developed an unsurpassed system of morality and religion, he confessed: "I apprehend it has received various corrupting Changes, and

I have some Doubts as to his Divinity; tho it is a question I do not dogmatize upon, having never studied it, and think it needless to bother myself with it now."[7]

Thomas Paine's description of the origins of Christian dogmas sums up what he, Franklin, and Jefferson had in common: a rejection of peculiar Christian dogmas still thought essential to salvation. "It is curious," Paine wrote,

> to observe how the theory of what is called the Christian Church sprung out of the tail of heathen mythology. A direct incorporation took place in the first instance, by making the reputed founder to be celestially begotten. The trinity of gods that then followed was no other than a reduction of the former plurality . . . the statue of Mary succeeded the statue of Diana of Ephesus; the deification of heroes changed into the canonization of the saints; the Mythologists had gods for everything; the Christian Mythologists had saints for everything; the Church became as crowded with the one as the Pantheon had been with the other, and Rome was the place for both. The Christian theory is little else than the idolatry of the ancient Mythologists, accommodated to the purposes of power and revenue; and it yet remains to reason and philosophy to abolish the amphibious fraud.[8]

In his discourse on the belief in divinely inspired scriptures, Paine punches an irreparable hole in the concept of scripturally "revealed" truth. He notes that every national religion pretends it is on a mission from God. Each religion has inspired founders and a holy book. Such books contain "revelations" which, he writes, indicate "something communicated *immediately* from God to man." Paine does not dispute the power of the Almighty to make such a communication but, he warns, admitting, for the sake of a case, that something has been revealed to a certain person, and not revealed to any other person, it is a revelation to that person only. When he tells it to a second person, a second to a third, a third to a fourth, and so on, it ceases to be a revelation to all those persons. It is a revelation to the first person only, and *hearsay* to every other, and, consequently, they are not obliged to believe it. ... It is a contradiction in terms and ideas to call anything a revelation that comes to us second-hand, either verbally or in writing. Revelation is necessarily limited to the first communication—after this it is only an account of something which that person says was a revelation made to him; and though he may find himself obliged to believe it, it cannot be incumbent on me to believe it in the same manner; for it was not a revelation made to me and *I* have only his word for it that it was made to him.[9]

The founding fathers' clear hostility to blind belief, recognizing the paramount harm it causes, creates a prescription for every American, it seems, to make, individually, an independent investigation of truth. Jefferson specifically called for such an investigation in the aforementioned letter to Peter Carr: "Fix reason firmly in her seat, and call to her tribunal every fact, every opinion." Therefore, it becomes all the more important to investigate at least two principal Christian doctrines, those of the atonement and of original sin, for these stand at the center of the fundamentalist holy of holies and, in my opinion, are the most subversive of inner harmony and social rectitude. Calling them effectively into question puts fundamentalists and other orthodox believers where they belong: in the category of cultists. I would ask Christian gay men and lesbians who seem unable to bear the thought of renouncing these doctrines, along with their straight-laced fellow creedists, to rethink what they have generally accepted without question.

Seasoned Christian scholars, including Derrick Sherwin Bailey, have examined the biblical account of Sodom and Gomorrah, and have discovered, they say, that it was not the "crime" of homosexual behavior for which these cities were reputedly destroyed, but because their inhabitants were found wanting in hospitality, a more serious offense in tribal times.[10] Gay MCC churches publish books and pamphlets that purportedly downgrade the importance of the Bible's six meager references to homosexuality, allowing Christian gay men and lesbians to declare without shame, as did MCC founder Perry in the title of his autobiography, *The Lord Is My Shepherd and He Knows I'm Gay*. They point out that Jesus himself never said one word about homosexuality, and that the Old Testament celebrates same-sex loves, including that between David and Jonathan and Ruth and Naomi. The particular "gay agenda" envisioned by MCC, therefore, involves not a tinkering with basic Christian dogmas, but, instead, an uncritical integration of same-sex lovers into mainstream theological trappings. My own approach runs counter to this tendency, which appears to me to be superficial.

Any minority that has experienced outcast status knows that self-esteem becomes, in its midst, an often elusive virtue. The great African-American sociologist W. E. B. Du Bois wrote that the worst effect of slavery and discrimination affecting his race, is that those discriminated against doubt themselves and share in a general contempt for others of their kind. As long as the members of any minority continue to internalize oppressor opinion, they will meekly accept negative ratings, failing to question the repressive thought system within which they dwell.

The "Christian" doctrine of Original Sin creates double jeopardy in this regard, offering, as it does, a negative take on human nature. Even if a gay person manages to upgrade his or her self-image, this doctrine remains as a reminder that he or she, because of Adam's transgression, is still a walking lump of depravity who must accept a second doctrine in order to avoid eternal outcast status. The second doctrine, The Atonement, has been called the scheme of redemption. It posits a "Christian" God who, at the supposed end of the Jewish era, was no longer moved by animal blood sacrifices for the "atonement of sins," and therefore demanded a perfect human blood sacrifice, namely Jesus. The early development of this doctrine prior to its emergence in "Christian" form, begs our understanding of its tribal uses in attempts to fashion behavioral tools. Nevertheless, the human sacrifice promulgated by early Christian theorists has developed it into a capitulation by modern-day human beings to a savage focus on blood sacrifices.

Belief in "Original Sin," Adam's unfortunate bequest to all humanity, has promoters in academic fields outside the scope of conventional religion. Biological determinists, for example, argue that the human race remains a captive of its animal heritage. The specimens they use to "prove" this theory are, generally, life forms lower on the evolutionary scale. Uncritical acceptance of such determinism allows little or no hope of elastic adaptability and change, and human beings are thereby condemned to repeat their errors on an increasingly large stage.[11] Fundamentalists are little bothered by this in any case, inasmuch as they hope to see fulfilled their interpretations of the Book of Revelations' prophecies of the end of the world and of the taking up of the faithful into heaven. Believing that their own souls will be saved as the worldwide carnage they predict erupts, provides them no reason to seek global reforms. This is an egocentric mind state that bypasses even cynicism in its dreadful social consequences.

Nevertheless, the corruption, evil, and depravity brought about by disobedience in the Garden of Eden did not stop the

Judaeo-Christian god from allowing a proliferation of Adamic descendants. After approximately fifteen hundred years, however, this god became so incensed over the behavior of his self-imaged creatures that, with the exception of eight persons, he drowned them all. The Hebrew god should have known, certainly, that his drownings were a useless endeavor. The remaining eight had been, like Adam and Eve, cursed by original sin. Once Noah's descendants reproduced, it was apparent that they were no better than those his god had drowned and so another scheme, it seemed, was needed. Thus far, when tribesmen transgressed Jehovah's law, they were required, by that same law, to sacrifice an animal, sharing with local priests its food revenue. Hopefully they also shared with those wronged. This procedure, a blood sacrifice, was turned into the unfortunate primitive fiction that "without the shedding of blood there is no remission of sins."[12]

The blood sacrifices of the Hebrew tribes thus encouraged the peculiar view that there is a specific connection between blood sacrifice and sin. The sacrifice of doves, for example, reportedly satisfied Jehovah's requirements for dealing with lesser transgressions. But as the transgressions multiplied, it became necessary to cut the throats of larger animals in order to rid the sinners of their guilt. Sheep and oxen were utilized and their meaty carcasses deposited in priestly pantries. Only through the sacrifice of the innocent could the guilty think themselves free of transgressive taint. The Christian theorists, while leaving Jewish customs behind, nevertheless enlarged the idea of sacrifice.

Sinning, not surprisingly, became such a widespread phenomenon, that—according to "Christian" doctrine—the sacrifice of animals was no longer sufficient as restitution. Since human beings lacked that innocence needed to make bloodletting "pure," only the sacrifice of God himself would do. If the planet was to be reclaimed, this doctrine teaches, it would be necessary for this god to die atoning for his creatures, all of whom were under the curse of his post-Adamic law. In a strange twist of justice, the ultimate Innocent would perish to save those guilty. It was as if a judge had recommended the execution of someone other than the actual murderer, calling such a miscarriage, as the "Christian" theoreticians call theirs, "satisfying the law." Jesus, alternately conceived as God, God's Son, and the Holy Ghost, was, in fact, the innocent human sacrifice that this god thought was needed.

If a believer in this scheme kills another because of misplaced values and an uncontrolled temper, he can rest easy thereafter, often waxing ecstatic as former "Christian" sinners do. The sin committed would be, theoretically, washed away in Jesus' blood. The more civilized ideas of restitution, of reparation, or some other attempt to undo the wrong committed gets pushed aside.

That a god would accept being tortured to wipe clean the records of various and sundry criminals destroys the central moral foundation on which any meaningful system of justice rests. This is most heinously accomplished by giving individuals a "quick fix" escape hatch from their sin, allowing them to consider sin *gone* instead of encouraging self-examination to search out misplaced internalized values that have caused the "sinner's" anti-social act. Whereas the born-again Christian fundamentalist would have us believe he is a patron of the good, society must be aware that he or she is not a product of earned virtue, but one who has been taught to think his *self* "saved" through a divinity's sacrifice rather than through a searching inner effort to perceive the actual state of the self. This fundamentalist deficiency lies at the very root of American society's disarray, giving reason to reconsider, perhaps, the predicament of those whom Socrates thought to be living worthless lives. "The unexamined life," he is reported to have said, "is not worth living."

A critic of Socrates once suggested that this statement of his was a bit harsh. But now, perhaps, it could easily be argued that such "harshness" is much needed as balance because the other route has been insanely glorified for so long. Those who dump their sins on an *invisible external power* fail to self-examine and have become, in fact, the prime subverters of a morally upright world by perpetuating self-ignorance, ignominiously swallowing unwholesome myths that propagate erroneous and savage doctrines.

In the next chapter I will explore how this lack of self-examination and dogmatism lead to intolerance and hatred of others seen as "different."

NOTES

1. Thomas Paine, *Age of Reason* (Amherst, N.Y.: Prometheus Books, 1984), p. 8.

2. A. Heron, *Towards A Quaker View of Sex* (London: Friends Home Service Committee, 1963).

3. Paine, *Age of Reason*, p. 8.

4. Thomas Jefferson, *The Life and Selected Writings of Thomas Jefferson*, ed. Adrian Koch and William Peden (New York: Modern Library, Random House, 1944), p. 47.

5. Ibid., p. 431.

6. Benjamin Franklin, *Writings* (New York: The Library of America, Library of Classics of the United States, 1987), p. 425.

7. Ibid., p. 1179.

8. Paine, *Age of Reason*, pp. 11–12.

9. Ibid., pp. 9–10.

10. Derrick Sherwin Bailey, *Homosexuality and the Western Christian Tradition* (New York: Longmans, Green, 1955).

11. "The 'aggressive violence' theories of Desmond Morris (*The Naked*

Ape), Konrad Lorenz (*On Aggression*), and Robert Ardery (*The Territorial Imperative*) have special appeal to many because they offer complacency. They can be accepted because they offer little hope for the future in these days of nuclear peril. A man need not bother himself about upgrading his scene. Reform? Revolution? Why bother? It seems easier to continue to express at least a few of these less admirable habit patterns until we are eventually eliminated by hydrogen warfare. In the meantime such thinking leads to fascism because there is no doubt that others need to be controlled. To unshackle the masses, says such a philosophy, is to invite them to kill you." Jack Nichols, *Men's Liberation: A New Definition of Masculinity* (New York: Penguin, 1975), p. 70.

12. H. L. Mencken reports that in pre-Christian Mexico, the god Huitzilopochtli required even more drastic techniques: the blood sacrifices to him of 50,000 youths and maidens. Huitzilopochtli, like many mythological gods, had no human father. He emerged from the womb of a virtuous widowed mother who had allowed herself a somewhat inexplicable but intimate relationship with the sun. His brother, Tezcatilpoca, was second in command in ancient Mexican religious lore, requiring the blood sacrifice of only half as many Mexican believers. "But today," writes Mencken, "Huitzilopochtli is as magnificently forgotten as Allen G. Thurman." H. L. Mencken, "Memorial Service," in *Prejudices: A Selection* (New York: Vintage Books, 1958), pp. 143–44.

3

Fundamentalist Hate Mongering and Its Tragic Consequences

*Christians have burned each other quite persuaded
That all the Apostles would have done as they did.*

Lord Byron[1]

THE HISTORY OF the Judaeo-Christian-Islamic tradition is, in great part, a record of massacres, crusades, inquisitions, and holy wars. It has been the followers of these three world religions who have, in the names of their faiths, beheaded, maimed, tortured, hanged, burned, hunted, exiled, excommunicated, and imprisoned not only outspoken critics of their creeds but those who have merely expressed or have been accused of expressing minor doubts.

It was John Calvin, the founder of Presbyterianism, who burned Michael Servetus at the stake for the "crime" of differing with him on the question of the Trinity. In doing so, Calvin simply followed examples set by Grand Inquisitors acting on behalf of the Roman Catholic Church, who not only set fires under countless thousands deemed heretical, but employed thumb screws, stretch racks, iron maidens, and other instru-

49

ments to show how the Christians treated others as themselves. Their torture chambers were nothing more than precursors, they thought, to the eternal torment that would be meted out after death to the same unfortunate individuals.

Whence arose this virulent hatred of fellow beings? *The True Believer,* Eric Hoffer's brilliant analysis of the nature of mass movements, explains that "hatred is the most accessible and comprehensive of all unifying agents." Hoffer says:

> Mass movements can rise and spread without belief in a God, but never without a belief in a devil. Usually the strength of a mass movement is proportionate to the vividness and tangibility of its devil. When Hitler was asked whether he thought the Jew must be destroyed, he answered: "No. . . . We should then have to invent him. It is essential to have a tangible enemy, not merely an abstract one." (H. Rauschning, *Hitler Speaks,* 1940, p. 234)[2]

Such hatred and the resultant ill-treatment of fellow human beings throughout the centuries also originates, no doubt, from fundamentalist reflections on God's behavior as recorded in the scriptures. This deity, Jehovah, was much given to questionable tantrums, causing him first to recommend through Moses certain retaliatory measures that by comparison make Branch Davidian David Koresh, the fiery prophet of Waco, a minor league player indeed.

These particular retaliatory measures appear in the Book of Numbers, chapter 31, where the Old Testament's principal lawgiver followed God's avenging commands and delivered unmistakable Waco-style instructions to the children of Israel as to how they should dispose of a nomadic tribe they attacked, a tribe of shepherds from whom they lifted (verse 32) "six hundred thousand and seventy thousand and five thousand sheep." In verses 17 and 18 appears this exhortation recommending the kidnapping and preservation of young female virgins: "Now therefore, kill every male among the little ones, and kill every woman that hath known man by lying with him. But all the women children, that have not known a man by lying with him, keep alive for yourselves."

In the thirteenth chapter of Deuteronomy Jehovah gives a most "inspiring" prescription for the treatment of those who serve

> other gods, which thou hast not known, thou nor thy fathers; namely the gods of the people which are around about you, nigh unto thee, or far off from thee, from the one end of the earth even unto the other end of the earth. Thou shall not consent unto him nor harken unto him, neither shall thine eye pity him, neither shalt thou spare him, neither shalt thou conceal him. But thou shalt surely kill him; thine hand shall be first upon him to put him to death, and afterward the hand of all the people. And thou shalt stone him with stones that he die. (Deut. 13:6–10)

In Leviticus 18:22 and 20:13 the Lord of Israel, eager, perhaps, to increase the size of his chosen tribe, denies men, but, interestingly enough, not women, the right to behave homosexually. Those men who lie with other men as with a woman, he says, must also be killed. For those who practice religious liberty and/or male homosexuality the penalty is the same: death. To the fundamentalist, who is under an obligation, reportedly, to accept each word of the Bible as God's own, the equal penalties in both cases seem just. To "think" otherwise would be to downgrade the Lord's Word to "sometimes inspired" or "sometimes just," an unacceptable alternative for those who believe that the Bible contains nothing but absolute and unadulterated truth.

Fortunately, within the United States, Jehovah's sense of justice, even though it is preached widely on the Sabbath, has undergone modifications for the better. Unfortunately, however, half the states, particularly those in the southern "Bible Belt," proudly advertise barbaric sex laws that still reflect Jehovah's unscientific opinions, though his penalties for specific sexual acts have suffered what may seem to Him, embarrassing downsizing. The fundamentalists would (when convenient) restore Jehovah's harsh punishments if they were able. But since at present they cannot, they satisfy themselves by doing what they can to make life miserable for those living "unacceptable" lifestyles and espousing beliefs which conflict with their own interpretations of the scriptures. The resulting fracas evokes feelings of *déjà vu*, for the thirteenth century, perhaps. Reflecting on the meddling vengefulness of Jehovah's self-anointed stewards reminds one of the words of the doxology: "as it was in the beginning, it now and ever shall be."

In Ireland, despite a fragile cease-fire in 1995, Protestants and Catholics continue to kill one another with aplomb. In Bosnia, Christians cheerfully massacre Moslems, and the bodies of the slain, including those of women and children, have been piled high on the evening news. In India, fundamentalist Moslems kill Hindus and fundamentalist Hindus return the favor with equal enthusiasm. Recent warfare in Lebanon between Christians and Moslems resurrected the spirit of the Crusades. In Israel, Jews and Moslems, though of the same racial stock, seem eternally at odds. In Egypt and Algeria, fundamentalist Moslems are killing moderate Moslems, and in the former Soviet Union, Christians and Moslems have revived nasty pogroms. "Man is a Religious Animal," wrote Mark Twain. "He is the only Religious Animal. He is the only animal that has the True Religion—several of them. He is the only animal that loves his neighbor as himself and cuts his throat if his theology isn't straight."[3]

In the United States the religious right favors strict censorship of the arts and the manipulation of public education to ensure it promulgates traditional religious perspectives. Such manipulation often stems directly from anti-gay fears. Florida's Lake County School Board chairperson, Pat Hart, proposed policy additions that she hoped would reflect her "convictions about family values and love for country." Her proposals included instruction in multicultural education that put appreciation of American basic values in the foreground "as superior to other foreign or historic cultures." "Homosexuality," said Ms. Hart, "will not be taught as an appropriate alternative lifestyle." Finally, she demanded an end to school practices such as deep breathing, yoga, and meditation, fearing these activities have foreign religious significances.[4]

These tragic, limiting consequences of know-nothing fundamentalist bamboozlement are, sadly, just the tip of an iceberg. Underneath this tip lie vast hosts of even more deadly fundamentalist behaviors. Pope John Paul II, an ultraconservative in collusion with Protestant fundamentalists, acts politically to stir up international opposition to condoms. In the age of AIDS, an orthodox clergy would give (unless ecclesiastical pipe dreams of premarital chastity become, for all people, a reality) green lights to the deadly virus, causing mass infections. Opposition by fundamentalists to abortion and birth control leaves large parts of the world unprotected against the crisis of overpopulation, now recognized by all but themselves. Mass starvation and irreparable damage to the environment are the result.

Around issues of nonreproductive sex, fundamentalist strategists have rallied their troops in an all-out effort to strip citizens not only of free choice, but of basic human rights such as housing and employment. Aware that their crusade against abortion has, of late, fizzled, the religious right has turned its focus toward the homosexually inclined, fearing that if the gay and lesbian liberation movement is successful in obtaining equal rights, their major defense against the decay of the patriarchal gender system, the gay taboo, will go the way of the tyrannosaurus.

To maintain the taboo is to foster a continuing climate of discrimination, causing those affected to internalize fundamentalist prejudices. When a young person realizes that he or she has been duped by these prejudices, the first reaction is usually anger. The movement for gay and lesbian liberation grows in strength as greater numbers become aware of the magnitude of the hex and the hoax which conventional society has placed on them. Their motivation for joining may be to create a climate protective of other young people experiencing the kind of despair anti-gay notions arouse in them.

America's religious right can now claim its deserved position as the primary source of anti-gay bigotry. Its propaganda spews forth hate messages on an hourly basis to television audiences across the nation. If there were FCC prohibitions, such as already protect other minorities against the broadcasting of such viciousness, fundamentalist hate mongering would be confined to their meeting places alone. But, unfortunately, there are no federal laws, as yet, protecting gay men and lesbians from abuse. Though hate crimes against homosexuals have soared statistically in recent years while, at the same time, fundamentalist calls for the death penalty for homosexuals are regularly repeated on "Christian" TV networks, the governing bodies of the United States have not yet been moved to offer much-needed federal protection on the basis of sexual orientation, thus leaving a large percentage of its citizenry at serious risk of injury, murder, job loss, and housing discrimination.

What is most regrettable, from the standpoint of the sexual majority, is that gay men and lesbians are their friends, children, brothers, sisters, favorite cousins, aunts, and uncles. Worse, the effect of discrimination has rebounded on the heads of the majority itself. Because it has failed to move quickly to protect the rights of others, it finds itself in harm's way. This became particularly clear to me when, in 1986, I met with the president of the Florida state senate, John Vogt, begging him to use his influence to increase awareness and prevention of AIDS in what was already a state ranked third in AIDS infections. "This is not a gay disease," I pleaded, but the state senate president showed little concern. "As long as the senate perceives this as a minority problem," he told me, "it will not be likely to act." Preventive education, therefore, lagged behind the times, causing death and disease irrespective of sexual orientation.

As the fundamentalist hate machine continues to publicly condemn homosexual feelings, suicide rates among distraught gay teenagers have jumped alarmingly. Major studies (Alan Bell and Weinberg, 1978; Karla Jay and Allen Young, 1979; Eric E. Rofes, 1983; Paul Gibson, 1989; T. L. Hammelman, 1993; Gary Remafedi, 1994; Joyce Hunter, 1994; Massachusetts Governor's Commission on Gay and Lesbian Youth, 1994; Curtis Proctor and Victor Groze, 1994)[5] estimate that one-third or more of all teen suicides are gay. Because of the closet factor, however, many experts consider this percentage low, indicating that because of underreporting, the number is probably closer to one-half. No matter which number proves correct, any percentage of such suicides is a national tragedy, one which is wildly exacerbated by anti-gay fundamentalist proselytizing. While more civilized citizens have shown their concern, young people in all fifty states, especially in smaller towns, have little access to such compassion and open-mindedness.

Mel White, the gay-identified author of *Stranger at the Gate:*

To Be Gay and Christian in America, and a former writer for hire for both Pat Robertson and Jerry Falwell, talks in his memoir of the sexual confusions his fundamentalist religious upbringing caused, tempting him, when he was a high school student, to suicide:

> When you are young and terrified by your impossible choices, you sometimes think it's better to die. I remember those nights alone when I toyed with walking into the surf or driving my jeep off a mountain road just to end the loneliness. . . . Thank God, I didn't give in to those thoughts of death when there was so much life ahead for me.[6]

Describing the vile level on which "religious" fundamentalists attempt to whip up anti-gay sentiment, *The Orlando Sentinel* quoted the venomous anti-gay rantings of a Sunday morning preacher: "They are like rats, skulking in their closets, copulating in mad frenzies, unable to control their sexual appetites, sniffing around the doors of school classrooms for fresh prey. Young prey. They are perverts and hedonists and spread disease like rats once spread the Black Plague. They will make fine kindling in Hell. But before then, before God gives them what they really deserve, they must be stopped here on Earth."[7] Pope John Paul II made reference to the scriptural death penalties for homosexuals in a 1986 letter: "In Leviticus 18:22 and 20:13, in the course of describing the conditions necessary for belonging to the Chosen People, the author excludes from the People of God those who behave in a homosexual fashion."

A letter from the Vatican, intercepted and published in the *Washington Post,* ordered American bishops to oppose legislation that promotes civil rights for gay men and lesbians, labeling homosexuality, in opposition to the American Psychiatric

Association's assessment, "an objective disorder." The *Post* said that the Roman Catholic Church has declared its support "for discrimination against gay people in such areas as public housing, family health benefits, and the hiring of teachers, coaches, and military personnel." The Vatican, it reported, insinuates that homosexuals are mentally ill and insists that the denial of rights to gays will promote family values. "The church has the responsibility," says the letter, "to promote public morality of the entire civil society on the basis of fundamental moral values." The rights to housing and employment, continues the missive, are not absolute, and employment, it says curiously, is "a privilege."[8]

Fortunately governments more civilized than the Vatican have ignored its devious ploys, while John Paul II has upped the ante in his war on gay men and lesbians worldwide. In a homily marked by fury, he attacked the European Parliament for its nonbinding resolution recommending that gay and lesbian couples be granted marriage and adoption rights. The resolution, in spite of the pope's previous warnings, had been passed 159–96 on February 8, 1994. It inappropriately conferred, said the pope, "institutional value on deviant behavior." Though Vatican attacks on political bodies are rare, the pontiff departed from his prepared text and, his voice rising in alarm, pontificated thusly: "A relationship between two men or two women cannot make up a real family."

At the same time that it waxes shrill in its attack on the world's homosexual communities, the Vatican is presently attempting, through confessing its long-standing sins, to patch up its centuries-old conflict with the Jews. Though Pope John Paul II has tried to distance himself from a document drafted by German and Polish bishops (acknowledging Catholicism's role in fostering centuries of anti-Semitism, pointing an accusatory finger at the Church of Rome for its failure to stop

the Holocaust and, in fact, recommending "an express con-
fession . . . of co-responsibility and guilt for the Holocaust"),
he cannot erase the historic facts on which his bishops make
their case. The document states that "the tradition of theological and church anti-Judaism was an important element on
the way toward the Holocaust."[9] Having thus lost the unifying
"hate" force provided by its embarrassing anti- Semitic stance,
the Holy See has stepped up its vilification of homosexuals,
aware, as Eric Hoffer's analysis might suggest, that tangible
devils are needed to stir mass reactions against those whom,
for its own strategic needs, it targets.

In a number of nations where Roman Catholic influence
predominates, the vicious persecution of gay men and lesbians
presently violates the most basic elements in any feasible con-
struct of human rights. Colombia can be singled out as a prime
exemplar of how homosexuals would be treated in a world gov-
erned by the pope. In Bogata routine raids on a variety of
meeting places, including those of gay liberationists, land gay
men in jail. Disappearances, beatings, torture, rape, and defa-
mation are their lot, assuring that the gay subculture lives perpetually in a state of terror. Amnesty International, the watch-
dog group that traces the crimes of nation-states against political prisoners, added the plight of gay men and lesbians in
Colombia and elsewhere to its list of concerns.

▼ ▼ ▼

In the United States, as elsewhere, the "crime" with which gay
citizens are charged is called "sodomy," deriving from the Old
Testament story of Sodom. A long-standing misinterpretation
of the reason Jehovah reputedly destroyed this city, namely,
that its inhabitants were "guilty" of same-sex attraction, has
been shown, however, to be erroneous by biblical scholars;

indeed, that no other Old Testament figure saw this tale in a homosexual light. Isaiah says Sodom was destroyed because its inhabitants were unjust (Isa. 1:10, 3–9). Jeremiah (23:14) laments the Sodomites' lying, adultery, and disinclination to repent. Ezekiel (16:49) claims that the Sodomites neglected the poor and had become proud and overly wealthy. In the Christian scriptures Jesus refers to Sodom's inhospitality, not its sexual practices (Matt. 10:15). St. Paul makes no mention of Sodom, while St. Peter refers only to the city's ungodliness. Excepting Jude, no "prophet" or saint, therefore, saw Sodom's "sin" in the same light as did the later church fathers. Jude, a twenty-five-verse New Testament tract, does make a vague connection (verse 7) between Sodom and "unnatural lusts," saying its inhabitants paid the penalty in eternal fire, though "most scholars believe that the style, content and probable date of this tract (late first or early second century) require the conclusion that Jude's name has been used by a letter writer to lend authority to his urgent appeal."[10]

Much the same kind of misinterpretation was attached to the Genesis story of Onan (Gen. 38:1–12), who was quickly dispatched by Jehovah after spilling his seed on the ground. This story has opened the door for opportunistic churches to condemn and manipulate the "sin" of masturbation, the most universally practiced of all sexual acts. A careful reading, however, shows that their interpretation is very much up for grabs. Onan was resisting Jehovah's law which required of him that he impregnate his dead brother's wife in order to keep the family line alive. It was not the "crime" of masturbation that infuriated an overreacting deity, but Onan's understandable refusal to sire a child by a woman who was not, in fact, his own wife. In any case, whether the story is of Sodom or of Onan, their relevance to meaningful morality is on a level (except for their lack of entertainment value) with narratives in *The Arabian Nights*.

Both biblical accounts have been used to maintain church thought-control over otherwise harmless and often beneficial sexual acts, unwholesomely casting them in a dark light, and inflicting on untold millions tragic, self-destructive guilt.

Since the public school system fails to impart to students much-needed methods of inquiry and critical thinking, absolutist fundamentalist fancies grow unhindered. Throughout the United States fundamentalists are running "stealth" campaigns for office as local educational or governmental bureaucrats. A surprising number of local school boards have fallen under their control. Such takeovers, inspired as they are by such a highly questionable religious ideology, are a direct threat to the American educational system.

Nearly three-quarters of a century after the famous Scopes "Monkey Trial," the fundamentalists are still promoting, wherever possible, their contrary view of origins, *creationism,* the doctrine that planet Earth came into existence less than six thousand years ago. This is a doctrine palatable only to the gullible, those who avoid accumulated knowledge and are ill equipped to ask basic questions. Only in an educational system where basic philosophical questions are left unspoken can the weeds of fundamentalist ignorance grow. Like creeping vines they move to cover and blight everything, including the acceptance of what they refer to disparagingly as "alternative" and therefore "deviant" lifestyles.

▼ ▼ ▼

As mentioned in chapter 2, certain doctrines of the religious right destroy self-examination as a basis for personal reformation, substituting instead the hypothesis of instantly "washed away sins" which in practice seldom seems to ask much more in the way of needed inward reflection. This creates a strange sort of zombie, potentially violent because of society's sexual repressions, often driven by bogus guilt and fears of everlasting torment, and yet brain-dead when it comes to asking those relevant questions that might lead to his or her self-reclamation. Criminality is simplified by the religious right with two narrow and ineffective approaches: civil punishment and the possibility of divine forgiveness. The abusive aspect of being "born again" because "saved by the blood," allows converts transgressions that are wiped miraculously clean and, *voilà*, the unpleasant "sins" are thereafter forgotten. Some may deny this but, in practice, thinking about inner motivations, especially when such thinking requires remembering gruesome acts, would eliminate the ecstatic high a convert seeks in the experience of being "saved." Those who favor the "washed away" approach argue that effective self-examination is not always possible. Although this may be true, is it not better that simple self-awareness reign as a principal social ideal than that it be misplaced in favor of a fundamentalist and orthodox emphasis too quickly exulting in the washing away of all sins?

The religious right focuses on its perception of what is good by teaching through prohibitions. This approach thus eliminates all focus on a personal discovery of the good by defining it in negatives. Do not doubt. Do not dance. Do not smoke. Do not drink. Do not feel lust. Do not have premarital intercourse. Do not swear. Do not masturbate. Do not skip church. And, of course, do not make love to anyone of the same gender. The tragedy's reach is clear, not only for same-sex lovers but for all living in any society where a much-needed search for the good, the true, and the beautiful has been heisted and effectively overridden by a paranoid emphasis on what people must not do.

In keeping with its system of prohibitions the religious right has launched a worldwide crusade to turn back the reproductive clock to the Victorian era. The reason for this is that the control of erotic matters enables orthodoxy to use sexual guilt to keep its cohorts unsuitably occupied with a multitude of personal infractions, not only actual but imagined. To lust in one's heart, they teach deliberately, is equal to committing authentic iniquities. Since, according to studies, sexual thoughts occur to men and women within five-minute intervals, sex becomes, for those who suffer under these cruel restrictions, a constant moral preoccupation. Clergy, "religious" political organizations, "Christian" political activists, and televangelists who use abortion and homosexuality to mobilize their troops and to appeal for monies used to increase their visibility on these two issues, include the emissaries of the Vatican as well as Jerry Falwell; Pat Robertson; D. James Kennedy; Charles Colson, convicted in the Watergate scandal; Tim LaHaye (Capital Report); Beverly LaHaye (Concerned Women for America); Gary Bauer (Family Research Council); Ralph Reed (and the Christian Coalition); R. J. Rushdoony; the Christian Action Network; American Security Council; Christian Life Coalition; the Ramsey Colloquium; Rutherford Institute; American Family Association; Operation Rescue; Eagle Forum; Citizens for Excellence in Education; Free Congress Foundation; and their many affiliates in various states.

Thus, tragically, more significant ethical issues are swept under a rug of ignorance where orthodox adults worry little about the living, and more about "the unborn." They focus not upon celebrating human love irrespective of gender, but upon hysterical condemnation of any love that does not fit within the confines of their particular doctrine. Their stake in the old dogmas is obvious: psychological control by orthodox churches is possible only if believers are inordinately preoccupied by sex.

Fanatical religious crusaders waging fierce local battles

over reproductive rights and homosexuality politicize vulnerable states where they play the lucrative homophobic card. Homosexuals, like the Jews of the Nazi era, are being blamed for every social evil, accused of causing, according to the mistaken orthodox twist on the Sodom story, the downfall of every civilization. To persons living in more sophisticated areas, such foul strategies are apparent; but in backwoods locales it is easy to appeal to prejudgments and fears, especially if they are linked to sex. In the eyes of wary Europeans, America continues to sustain an anti-sexual zeal unequaled elsewhere. It is this zeal which feeds the fundamentalists' anti-gay campaigns.

Where enlightened city commissions have passed local ordinances protecting gay men and lesbians from hateful and discriminatory practices in such areas as employment and housing, the vindictive religious right has stepped in to mobilize a repeal of these protections by calling them, falsely, "special rights." The U.S. Supreme Court decision *Romer* v. *Evans* (May 20, 1996), however, may have put a stop to these initiatives and to constitutional amendments such as Colorado's Amendment 2, backed by the Christian right wing group Colorado for Family Values. Their initially triumphant passage of their anti-gay amendment had ramifications throughout the nation. But because of the Supreme Court's decision against them, a nightmare blanket denial of rights to gays and lesbians is no longer possible. The Supreme Court majority said: "We must conclude that Amendment 2 classifies homosexuals not to further a proper legislative end but to make them unequal to everyone else. This Colorado cannot do."

This legal victory affecting lesbian and gay men in their struggles against the fundamentalists is truly historic, though it should not be a cause in America for complacency. The fundamentalists still hold startling hands of meddlesome cards which they will play with unrelenting zeal. "It is provided in the essence of things," writes Walt Whitman, "that from any fruition of success, no matter what, shall come forth something to make a greater struggle necessary."

NOTES

1. Lord Byron (George Gordon), "Don Juan," 1821, in *The Great Thoughts,* ed. George Seldes (New York: Ballantine Books, 1985), p. 63.

2. Eric Hoffer, *The True Believer* (New York: Harper & Row, 1951).

3. Mark Twain, "The Damned Human Race," in *The Great Thoughts,* p. 83

4. Rick Badie, "Lake School Board Chairwoman Tries to Limit Gay, Multicultural Education," *Orlando Sentinel,* June 11, 1993, p. B–1

5. Linnea Due, *Joining the Tribe: Growing Up Gay and Lesbian in the '90s* (New York: Anchor Books, Doubleday, 1995), p. xxxvi.

6. Mel White, *Stranger at the Gate: To Be Gay and Christian in America* (New York: Simon and Schuster, 1994), p. 52

7. Mike Thomas, "Are Gay Rights a Civil Right?" *Florida* (magazine), *Orlando Sentinel,* July 18, 1993, p. 8.

8. Gustav Niebuhr, "Two Bishops Sign Ad Backing Gay Rights: Clerics Join in Public Statement Responding to the Vatican's Stand," *Washington Post,* November 1, 1992, p. A–4. Also Thomas C. Fox, *Sexuality and Catholicism* (New York: George Braziller, Inc., 1995), p. 149.

9. Associated Press, "Anti-Semitism Report Is a Hot Potato for Vatican," *Miami Herald,* May 27, 1994, p. 17–A.

10. *New English Bible, Oxford Study Edition,* p. 309.

Homosexuality and the Equality of the Sexes

The Female equally with the Male I sing.
Walt Whitman[1]

THE RAMSEY COLLOQUIUM, a group of Christian and Jewish scholars sponsored by the Institute on Religion and Public Life, is as well a conservative ecumenical theological "think" tank. In the March 1994 issue of *First Things*, the Colloquium launched a dogmatic assault on the gay and lesbian liberation movement, linking it to "radical feminism."[2] Though the foremost mainstream feminist group, the National Organization for Women (NOW), can hardly be called "radical," a link between gay liberation and feminism does undeniably exist. Molly Yard, a former NOW president, and Urvashi Vaid, former executive director of the National Gay and Lesbian Task Force, issued simultaneous statements making their organizations unabashed allies in the struggle for sexual equality.[3]

Just as society begins to acknowledge defects in its old-fashioned feminine model, so, too, must it come to grips with destructive strains in commonly accepted definitions of masculinity. Many of these definitions have their origins in earlier times and in the laws supposedly delivered by a patriarchal god "The Father," who often emerges alternately angry, jealous, and violent in the pages of the Old and New Testaments. Old definitions die hard, however, and powerful social forces, whose economic welfare is attached to the status quo, continue to foster standards favored by the politically active religious right. By encouraging divisive dual philosophies of thought and behavior, fundamentalists resist the strengths that would result from shared gender perspectives, segregating so-called male and female qualities and promoting the labeling of them as "opposites." For centuries St. Paul's advice that women must be silent and submissive, kept males supreme over their female "property." As times changed, however, the chattel got uppity, agitating to be allowed to vote, and thus creating the first wave of American feminism in the early part of this century. With the rise of late 1960s feminism (American feminism's second wave), the status quo was challenged, inspiring biblical literalists to become standard bearers of reactionism.

Even so, the cultural revolution of the 1960s subjected traditional feminine roles to an unrelenting assault. "Masculine" roles, however, bound to patriarchal biblical concepts promoting sexual inequality, have thus far undergone only minor modifications. There is now more of a tendency toward intellectual one-upmanship as opposed to earlier standards of mere physical domination. In any case, the supposed supreme value placed on being a controlling agent remains, unfortunately, too common among men, even while the male provider role seems to be dissolving rapidly, as more and more women, because of economic necessity, enter the work force. Sadly, most men are not well prepared for this diminution of their traditional protector role. Violence as a male solution and the "sacred" place in America accorded the value of competition keeps individual males from appreciating the social importance of cooperation. The old male roles clearly make conventionally conditioned men dangerous to themselves and to women, and the homosexual taboo has served as a major defense against any storming of these antiquated "masculine" codes. "If you do such and such, you are a sissy," youthful males are warned. Once the antigay taboo dissolves, there will be a greater likelihood that men, especially those who become heterosexually inclined, can then partake of nurturant values once thought proper for women alone. With the gay taboo gone, and feminine equality assured, there will be no epithets like "sissy" or "queer" to frighten men into conformist and oppressive "masculine" straitjackets.

While women, lesbian women, and gay men suffer second-class status under established religious, political, and commercial rulings about "proper" behavior between the sexes, there is a minor divergence between feminism and gay liberation created by the fact that heterosexually inclined women are integrated into society provided they follow archaic demands that they remain subordinate. If they do not, they are given pejorative labels, the "worst" being that which lumps them with lesbians. This is because these autonomous women desire to be fully independent and yet loving, as opposed to biblical injunctions that they must be loving only if they are relegated to an inferior ranking, in thought and deed, to males. But gay men and lesbians are relegated to wholesale outcast status by virtue of being considered, under the gender system requiring male control, altogether improper. Since the labels "dyke" or "faggot" continue as the only remaining vilifications by which those who disobey the gender system are tarnished, feminists have discovered that it is as important to their cause that these abusive terms die as it is to the individuals against whom the terms are directed.

American feminism, especially in its earlier stages, has not always been aware of its link to gay and lesbian liberation. One who sided with the prejudices of the religious right was Betty Friedan, whose book *The Feminine Mystique* helped inspire women in the 1960s and 1970s. Friedan harbored prejudices against the homosexually inclined which differed little from fundamentalist propagandists. Her first reaction to lesbians was to label them a menace. Within the ranks of NOW, an organization she helped found, she exerted no little effort to dislodge lesbian women from power positions in the movement whose prophetess she thought herself to be. Pioneering gay journalist and editor Mark Thompson says in his twenty-five-year history, *Long Road to Freedom*, that "a year after National Organization for Women (NOW) founder Betty Friedan called lesbians a threat to the women's movement, a resolution supporting lesbian rights was withdrawn during NOW's convention because the national committee judged it too controversial. On the opening night of the National Congress to Unite Women, twenty-five women wearing T-shirts emblazoned with the words LAVENDER MENACE—Friedan's slur of choice—took over the stage."[4]

When the cause of men's liberation emerged in the mid–1970s, Friedan took immediate sides with avowedly heterosexual male proponents. Presented by homosexual theoreticians with major works dissecting masculine roles, Friedan, safe in her cocoon, ignored them. She showed no knowledge of earlier feminists such as Emma Goldman (1869–1940), whose sympathies went out to the despised gay minority. Goldman had said:

> I regard it as a tragedy that people of a differing sexual orientation find themselves proscribed in a world that has so little understanding for homosexuals and that displays such

gross indifference for sexual gradations and variations and the great significance they have for living. It is completely foreign to me to wish to regard such people as less valuable, less moral, incapable of noble sentiments and behavior.[5]

Long before Ms. Friedan's arrival on the scene, nineteenth-century visionaries like Walt Whitman and Edward Carpenter had made those connections between feminism and homosexuality which she failed to do. The opening verse in Whitman's *Leaves of Grass* celebrates gender equality and Edward Carpenter's book *Love's Coming of Age* (1896)[6] also linked the fortunes of oppressed subordinates, both male and female. Carpenter foresaw a future in which an alliance between gay liberation and feminism was inevitable.

Prior to the arrival of 1960s feminism, women's liberationists had focused mainly on gaining access to bastions of male power, which might allow them an equal voice in matters affecting themselves and society. As they sought the vote and moved slowly but surely into educational fields, assuring themselves equal opportunities as skilled laborers, they hoped, too, for an unprecedented say in the intellectual and cultural life of society. Until the 1960s, however, there had never been a questioning of traditional roles like housekeeping, motherhood, and child care. The 1960s stage of the gender revolt introduced demands for alternatives to "women's work," suggesting that femininity need not be linked to traditional roles. Child rearing, household cleaning, and the preparation of meals would, of necessity, be regarded as men's work, too.

The effect of this was, at first, a subliminal realization that there also exists a need for the challenging of male roles. It was under the influence of this realization that some, including Myron Brenton (*The American Male*) and myself (*Men's Liberation: A New Definition of Masculinity*),[7] wrote about men's liberation, calling for a reexamination of what constitutes masculinity. If there are to be changes in women's roles, it was argued, there must be a commensurate change among men. These works examined male behaviors and saw the major disadvantages not only for women but for men as well, whether straight or gay-identified. It was clear, as the religious fundamentalists sensed, that persuading men of the illusions and pitfalls of their role-inspired aspirations to dominate and control would first require putting an end to anti-homosexual prejudices. At the 1976 annual meeting of the American Sociological Association, speakers noted that conventional male roles are taught early. Studies show that boys, unlike girls, know what is expected of them by the time they are in kindergarten. Girls amble gradually, for at least five more years, in the direction of socially prescribed feminine patterns. Harshly enforced, masculinism is taught in negatives; a boy's role is inculcated by trainers holding up the terrible scarecrow: the sissy, which frightens him more than does the threat of hell fire. His peers, lacking information about masculinity superior to his own, reinforce such fears. He listens to them. The blind lead the blind, walking with anxieties caused by prohibitions that were imposed in preschool environments. Young males and their friends end with oversimplified visions of manliness to which they cling. Denying all feminine identifications, they live their lives disowning a major part of the psyche.

Both gay liberation and feminism seek for those represented the self-confidence that develops when an individual realizes his or her equal status. After the famed 1969 Stonewall uprising which marked the media's awareness of "gay power," poet Allen Ginsberg spoke in the *Village Voice* of the new homosexuals and contrasted them with those remembered from a decade earlier. "They no longer have that 'wounded' look," he said.[8] Within the last quarter century there has emerged the new woman similarly poised. Her posture is changing. Instead of simpering subordination, she now projects an egalitarian stance. As men and women experience without fear those virtues once thought proper only to the "opposite" gender, such self-assurance will co-exist (in both sexes) and a free interplay of revealing emotional expressions will light faces in truthful splendor. Already there are indications that mincing gaits are turning into bolder steps. Aerobics trainers, body builders, and, in public schools, coaches who assure equal access to athletics programs, abound. The female form is beginning to reflect the new woman's commitment to regular exercising, providing her countenance with signs of energetic health, as opposed to harmful face painting with chemically based makeup.

In his pioneering work on homosexuality, *The Intermediate Sex* (1908), Edward Carpenter argued for a "melding" of the sexes:

> If the modern woman is a little more masculine in some ways than her predecessor, the modern man (it is to be hoped), while by no means effeminate, is a little more sensitive in temperament and artistic in feeling than the original John Bull. It is beginning to be recognized that the sexes do not or should not normally form two groups hopelessly isolated in habit and feeling from each other, but that they rather represent the two poles of *one* group—which is the human race; so that while certainly the extreme specimens at either pole are vastly divergent, there are great numbers in the middle region who (though differing corporeally as men and women) are by emotion and temperament very near to each other. We all know women with a strong dash of the masculine temperament, and we all know men whose almost feminine sensibility and intuition seem to belie their bodily form. Nature, it might appear, in mixing the ele-

ments which go to compose each individual, does not always keep her two groups of ingredients—which represent the two sexes—properly apart, but often throws them crosswise in a somewhat baffling manner, now this way and now that; yet wisely, we must think—for if a severe distinction of elements were always maintained the two sexes would soon drift into far latitudes and absolutely cease to understand each other.[9]

As the new 1960s woman rejected long-established gender roles, she reacted angrily to resulting charges of *inadequacy*. Not surprisingly, many gay liberationists were able to understand her anger. Knowing from bitter experience how prejudices spread, inflamed by simple-minded masculine and feminine stereotypes labeling gays and lesbians "half men" and "bull-women," they identified with feminism's call for the abolition of a gender system which, in its insecurity, relies on such insults. Indeed, some gay men struck back by overreacting or counterreacting, donning leather costumes to accentuate "masculinity." In the wake of accusations that they were "sissies" or "effeminates," such clothing helped them prove themselves to be "just as masculine as the next guy." Most of these reactionaries little realized that "the next guy" was, with the simultaneous emergence of feminist awareness, struggling in almost equal measure with concerns relating to his "masculine" image.

At the other end of the mannerism pole, males, straight and gay, after enduring ridicule because of what were perceived as their feminine traits, accentuated their femininity. The transvestite and transsexual wings of the gender revolt produced a variety of types who unashamedly emphasized their rejection of the macho straitjacket by wearing traditional female attire. The lesbian counterparts of these extremes were popularly identified as "masculine" leather-wearing Dykes on Bikes, or as those nicknamed Lipstick Lesbians, who clung to old-fashioned feminine artifacts and attire. Sheila Sullivan, a transvestite who reflected on early 1970s calls for "unisex" or "androgyny" that looked forward to a world in which feminine males or masculine women would be accepted as such, pointed out that

> it is putting the cart before the horse to expect transvestites to assist, or even participate, in "unisex" or other socially acceptable avenues for the expression of male femininity. Society has made itself quite clear to the transvestite that he is freer as an undetected, disguised woman-man than as an effeminate man. Transvestites are victims of societal sex roles and until these roles become disassociated from one's actual biological sex, we will continue to produce transvestites. The sure sign of a totally role-liberated society will be the absence of future-generation "transvestites," and the existence of healthy and free feminine men.[10]

A majority of gay men and lesbians are outwardly indistinguishable from their straight counterparts partly because commercial enterprises promoting masculine and feminine stereotypes offer fashionable clothing and products appropriate to yesteryear's gender prescriptions. Among men certain images still exert an extraordinary appeal, as evidenced by the popularity of violent sports and the exploits of supermacho film stars. Women's images continue along a retrogressive curve celebrated in magazines like *Cosmopolitan*.

These images reinforce inequities unknown in certain South Sea islands like Vanatinai, where egalitarian sex roles persist. On Vanatinai, where there exist no pronouns like "he" or "she," siblings, both male and female, care for children and fathers are also expected to share the burden. Women, unlike those bound in the Judaeo-Christian tradition, enjoy the same sexual rights and freedoms as men. There are no "male cult" activities and no "males only" clubs. According to the research of anthropologist Maria Lepowsky, decision making and the holding of property seem, in practice, to bear no relationship to gender. Women, explains Dr. Lepowsky, can inherit and own land. Instead of lifelong monogamy, individual males and females are expected to mate several times before settling into prolonged relationships. Worshiping both male and female gods, women, in contrast to those sequestered by fundamentalist Christian dogma, have full access to the supernatural. They share with men knowledge of magical spells, incantations, and rituals.

In recent times the transformation of the warrior role has been partially extended, in several nations, to women. In the United States the new woman has taken major steps to gain greater and more responsible military status, but in stages begrudged her by the male brass, who resist her penetration into the previously sacrosanct domain of male combatants.

World War II saw significant advances by women who wished to perform military service, but not until a half century later have women's gains expanded and solidified. Each step taken has been surrounded with controversy. Since men consider combat their own peculiar province, the macho distinction they have previously enjoyed is eliminated as the "opposite" sex stands next to them on the battlefield. This changeover has been made easier for them to swallow, however, due to the decades-long history of women's distinguished service just short of the combat zone. Women's ministrations as nurses have been accepted since Florence Nightingale traversed the front lines. The services performed by gay men, however, as combatants and nurses, have been acceptable only so long as they have remained closeted. The fury surrounding President Clinton's failed attempt to fully integrate homosexually inclined persons into the military originates in the role-conditioned male's extreme resistance to any further opening of the door into his last bastion of "masculine" differentiation, and his subliminal awareness that the singular division of labor by which his culturally induced role is protected is crumbling.

He fails to appreciate that scientific advances have altogether changed the state of warfare, placing much of its application at the controls of technology, a gender-neutral domain. Warfare, with the onset of the nuclear age, is now very much a questionable option. Human continuance now requires a conscious reexamination of the value of male dominance through the use of "manly" force, and the presumptive protective blanket that this role-inculcated consciousness is said to throw across the whole of society. His defensive readiness to fight makes the macho man, in fact, a threat to human continuance, and his inability to care for his fellow man, in the most esteemed and loving sense, turns him, like some outraged jealous jungle beast, into a creature even more dangerous. His male role conditioning finds him approaching his fellows in competitive frameworks, racing to get ahead rather than cooperating for mutual gratification. His sexual/affectional life is especially competitive since, on a deeper level, he sees other men as rivals. This factor has its roots partly in capitalist notions of possession, in which women, like cattle or flashy automobiles, are considered property. An unchecked heterosexuality approached in this manner, as long as it is considered the norm, encourages contention.

Many early anti-militaristic counterculture communes of the 1960s were said to falter primarily because of jealousy among male rivals competing for exclusive rights of sexual access. Since this occurred in a time frame mostly predating women's second public round of social self-examination, male commune members had little awareness of alternative possibilities. Even so, when they engaged in communal heterosexual sex, certain conscious advances occurred. When they were positioned next to other males, men's fears of contact with those males were somewhat alleviated and, for a time, a phenomenon called "bisexual chic" was touted by media. Bisexuality, as opposed to exclusive heterosexuality or homosexuality, was regarded by counterculture youths as a more flexible and encompassing approach to relationships. Joseph Epstein, writing in *Harper's* magazine in 1970, described his shock after he'd asked his long-haired seventeen-year-old straight hippie stepson what he knew of "the new homosexuals." "If you mean guys buggering each other," replied the boy, "it goes on all the time, and drugs don't necessarily have to be involved. 'You scratch my back and I'll scratch yours,' is kinda how guys see it."[11]

Such a statement evokes horror within fundamentalist circles. It seems clear to the fundamentalists that homosexuality can be made attractive to the impressionable. Thus, commentaries such as Joseph Epstein's are indicative of their foremost fear, namely, the "prairie fire effect" of homosexuality, and they see conversion from heterosexual patterns a distinct possibility if there is no protective taboo. Feminist critiques of the nuclear family arrangement add extra angst, foreshadowing basic changes in human conduct that overthrow the primitive doctrines on which old social patterns rest.

Since feminism and gay liberation can pose alternatives to behaviors that conflict with biblical literalism, fundamentalist critics of these movements are correct when they say they undermine a much revered status quo. That gay men and lesbians, such as the pioneers Karl Heinrich Ulrichs (1825–1895)[12] and Jane Addams (1860–1935),[13] have often stood as pivotal figures, prominent theoreticians and foremost leaders in the feminist and men's liberation causes does nothing less than fulfill the amazing prophecies of Edward Carpenter made a century ago:

> It is possible that the Uranian [gay*] spirit may lead to something like a general enthusiasm of Humanity, and that the Uranian people may be destined to form the advance guard of that great movement, which will one day transform the common life by substituting the bond of personal affection and compassion for the monetary, legal and other external ties which now control and confine society. Such a part, of course, we cannot expect the Uranians to play unless the capacity for their kind of attachment also exists, though in a germinal and undeveloped state, in the breast of mankind at large. And modern thought and investigation are clearly tending that way—to confirm that it does so exist.[14]

A most significant concern of conservative fundamentalists who, in the 1960s, opposed men's growing of long hair was that such a development would blur distinctions between the sexes. While this says little for their powers of observation, their basic fear becomes, in the context of this argument, clear. They were concerned that men might look on other men, possibly with lust, unable to take into account the distinctive qualities that formerly separated them from women and which maintained, therefore, the old patriarchal gender system. To the extent that Joseph Epstein's stepson's observations matched reality, fundamentalist fears about the weakening of those antiquated "Christian" social bonds to which they cling are, no doubt, well founded.

---

*"Uranian" was a term coined by Ulrichs to denote gay males. The term "homosexual" was coined by Karoly Maria Benkert (later Kertbeny) (1823–1882).

Many other factors enter into showing how feminism and gay liberation are linked. To build new societies graced by sexual equality will necessitate revolutionary changes in consciousness. Incorporation by both men and women of qualities once thought proper only to "opposite" sexes will strengthen rather than (as fundamentalists fear) weaken social bonds. In Edward Carpenter's long-ago vision stood a human being in whom the interplay of qualities, of strength and sensitivity, of rationalism and intuition, of nurturance in men and athleticism in women, would create a new kind of person meant, I think, to populate future centuries. The fundamentalists, however, would have us look backwards to specific doctrinal roots that deny the goodness of any sexual liaison which is not for the purpose of reproduction. For sparsely populated Middle Eastern tribes in millenniums past, perhaps such denials had roots in logic. But today, if only procreative sex is allowed, these uncut roots will turn into monster weeds strangling humanity's attempts to push forward toward new and necessary thresholds.

Nonprocreative same-sex relationships have a particularly redeeming quality, namely, that they take place between people who are *the same* and can therefore, theoretically at least, welcome others into affectional relations that bypass exclusivity. This, conceivably, could promote a maximization of affection through communal contact, replacing today's failing models of exclusive, neurotic, narrow, monogamous duos.

NOTES

1. Walt Whitman, "One's-Self I Sing," *Leaves of Grass* (Amherst, N.Y.: Prometheus Books, 1995), p. 9.

2. Ramsey Colloquium, *First Things*, March 1994, excerpted in the *Miami Herald*, March 11, 1994, p. 19.

3. Urvashi Vaid, *Virtual Equality: The Mainstreaming of Gay and Lesbian Liberation* (New York: Anchor Books, 1995), p. 117.

4. Mark Thompson, ed., *Long Road to Freedom: The Advocate History of the Gay and Lesbian Movement* (New York: St. Martin's Press, 1994), p. 37.

5. Leigh W. Rutledge, *Unnatural Quotations* (Boston: Alyson Publications, 1988), p. 112.

6. Edward Carpenter, "Love's Coming of Age," from *Selected Writings,* vol. 1, *Sex* (London: Gay Men's Press, 1984).

7. Myron Brenton, *The American Male* (New York: Fawcett World Library, 1966), and Jack Nichols, *Men's Liberation: A New Definition of Masculinity* (New York: Penguin Books, 1975).

8. Lucian Truscott, IV, "Gay Power Comes to Sheridan Square," *Village Voice,* July 3, 1969, p. 1.

9. Carpenter, "The Intermediate Sex," *Sex,* pp. 189–90.

10. Sheila "Lou" Sullivan, *Toward Transvestite Liberation: GPU News,* Milwaukee, February–March 1974.

11. Joseph Epstein, "Homo-Hetero: The Struggle for Sexual Identity," *Harper's,* September 1970, p. 51.

12. Karl Heinrich Ulrichs, *The Riddle of Man-Manly Love,* trans. Michael A. Lombardi-Nash, foreword by Vern L. Bullough (Amherst, N.Y.: Prometheus Books, 1994).

13. Paul Russell, *The Gay 100: A Ranking of the Most Influential Gay Men and Lesbians, Past and Present* (New York: Carol Publishing Group, 1995), p. 106.

14. Carpenter, "The Intermediate Sex," *Sex,* p. 238.

5

Major Fundamentalist Lies

Christmas songs talk about being adorned with gay apparel, God for-
bid! I'm so turned off by the word "gay," I won't even use Ben Gay!
Dallas evangelist James Robison[1]

PROPAGANDISTIC HATE FILMS touting a so-called gay agenda
have been produced and circulated widely by the religious
right. Each has been carefully edited so as to create false
impressions of gay men and lesbians as well as the "evil" social
program they are accused, en masse, of desiring. Fund-raising
letters, couched in inflammatory language to frighten recipi-
ents, are sent out over the signatures of ministers. They
promise to use the dollars sent to bring a halt to this imaginary
gay agenda, one, they say, that favors a variety of outrageous
proposals ranging from the "right" to molest children to a
fondness for spreading AIDS.

Recently, over a hundred gay Jews, representatives of
twelve nations, filed through a Jerusalem shrine honoring the
victims of Hitler's atrocities.[2] Orthodox Jews shouted curses at
them, wishing AIDS upon them, and evoking the death

penalty found in Leviticus 20:13: "If a man also lieth with mankind, as he lieth with a woman, both of them have committed an abomination: they shall surely be put to death."

If the Hebrew scriptures prescribed death, it was Hitler who followed to the letter the Levitican law. The social advances made by the German gay and lesbian movements of the early 1930s had been significant. Hitler used these advances, just as the religious right uses them now, to trumpet warnings that "the sky is falling," promising, while publicizing his hate agenda, to eliminate the "threat" forthwith. Not surprisingly, he opened, with Heinrich Himmler, a Reich Central Office for the Combating of Homosexuality and Abortion, in order to stir up, as does the religious right today, hatred against what Hitler labeled a "fringe" or marginalized minority.[3] Gay men and lesbians were branded with pink triangles before being forced, along with the Jews and other "undesirables," into the gas chambers. Himmler addressed the führer's storm troopers, saying, "if we continue to have this burden [of homosexuality] in Germany, without being able to fight it, then that is the end of Germany, and the end of the Germanic world."[4]

Consequently the Third Reich's henchmen burned Berlin's prestigious Institute for Sexual Science which had housed, for scholars and the public, thousands of volumes on the psychology, history, and physiology of gay men and lesbians. After coming to power Hitler waited less than a month before banning all gay-rights organizations. Most recently, in Jerusalem, the speaker of the Israeli parliament, responding to fundamentalists' scorning of fellow gay Jews, reminded these extremists that gay men and lesbians, too, had been Hitler's victims.

Never again," say survivors of Hitler's extermination camps. Sadly, "cleansing" crusades involving other minorities, including those in Bosnia, Rwanda, Turkey, and Sri Lanka, rage out of control. Ending these pogroms in concert with other nations allows the planet to experience its interconnectedness; to experience and understand the roots of the racial and sexual hysterics behind bigotry's cancerous growths, and thus to quash them.

In the United States, riding on fundamentalist approval, well-placed persons in the Republican Party whip up anti-gay hatreds and suspicions. Republican presidential hopefuls cater, to their party's detriment, to the fundamentalist fringe. Pat Buchanan, for example, uses homosexuals as bogeymen against whom he promises he will protect America. With the exception of one or two outstanding men, other GOP candidates celebrate homophobia to an unparalleled degree. Republican and religious right pundits like Cal Thomas compete with each other to be more homophobic than thou. In the immediate wake of their crusades, the religious right, hiding behind various front organizations such as Colorado for Family Values or The American Family Association (founded reputedly to protect the fundamentalist concept of "family"), spearhead campaigns across America, eager to eliminate, as Hitler did, all protections offered by local municipalities for gay citizens suffering hate crimes and employment discrimination. Presently fundamentalists are calling for a boycott of Disney because it offers, as do several other major corporations, benefits to same-sex couples among its employees. It was Pat Robertson's youthful cohort, Ralph Reed of the Christian Coalition, who asked Congress to help "Christians" whip up hysteria against gay marriages, calling for a proposed bill that would be code-named "Marriage Defense."[5] But does anyone seriously believe that the banning of same-sex marriages will protect opposite-sex marriages?

Organizations such as People for the American Way, the American Civil Liberties Union (ACLU), Amnesty International, the Human Rights Campaign Fund, and Americans United for Separation of Church and State make valiant attempts to stop these "Christian" maneuvers, but even President Clinton has said he would sign the fundamentalist-engineered Republican bill to outlaw same-sex-marriage, fearing, after his earlier gays-in-the-military fiasco, a second fight over a divisive issue germane mostly to openly gay and lesbian Christians nationwide. Nor does Clinton wish, as of this writing, to seem unfriendly to a congressional bill that boasts, however untruthfully, that it is "family supportive." Several significant "Christian" anti-gay initiatives, as a result, are now mushrooming into firmly entrenched political stances, and fundamentalists yearn to make them law, backed by peephole police and prisons. Such a development was predicted in 1955 by sociologists Dr. David Riesman and Nathan Glazer:

> Furthermore, the sexual emancipation which has made the Negro less of a feared and admired symbol of potency has presented men with a much more difficult problem: the fear of homosexuality. Indeed homosexuality becomes a much more feared enemy than the Negro. (It may be that homosexuality itself is spreading or news of it is spreading, so that people are presented with an issue which was formerly kept under cover—another consequence of enlightenment.) How powerful, then, is the political consequence of combining the image of the homosexual with the image of the intellectual—the State Department cooky-pusher Harvard trained sissy thus becomes *the focus* of social hatred. . . .[6]

If, in the United States, crime, disease, and unemployment continue to rise (which seems inevitable), Republican politicians are already using Nazi strategies to treat gay men and lesbians as scapegoats to mollify society's discontents. Congressman Robert Dornan (R.-Cal.), for example, as recorded in the Congressional Record, has found a way to harass and possibly ferret out gays in tirades about the Postal Service. "I hope the Postal Service realizes that sodomy is still illegal in most states; indeed, the Supreme Court has ruled that state laws against sodomy are perfectly constitutional."[7] Each local right wing zealot Republican returning to power means replays of such "moralizing" and hysteria. The religious right has already prepared the ground for such skullduggery, planting a multitude of lies destined to grow, with "religious" sanction, into whips and clubs designed for a long, painful season of gay-bashing.

American psychologist William James believed the human libido to be bisexual. He wrote that homosexuality is "a kind of sexual appetite of which very likely most men possess the germinal possibility." The average man, even though he may have experienced homosexual contacts, pushes memory of them from his mind, forgetting that such things ever occurred. The right wing has tapped into his psyche by magnifying the implied threat that comes with social equality for gay males. He fears that his emotions, or those of his children, may run helter skelter and who knows where? He must condemn gay men to prop up male-role conditioning, under which he slaves, as an ever-present reality in his own life. Remove the gay taboo and a flood of "unnatural" thoughts will frightfully dance across his psyche.

The religious right capitalizes, as it always has, on anxiety. In a day when sorcery, witchcraft, and devil possession have become antiquated concerns, homosexuals make for a visible substitute. Understanding homosexuality, both in oneself or in others, is a chore. It seems easier to condemn rather than, as Socrates recommends, to examine the self. When the church waxes hot in its condemnation, it becomes difficult to stand in its way, often for fear of being associated with those it condemns. The gay minority gets stereotyped through its cynical manipulation of negative images.

The first argument used by religious fundamentalists to justify their anti-gay position is that homosexuality is against nature. While cursory studies of zoology and anthropology contradict this assertion, those who use it fail to see that the acts they condemn, including oral and anal sex, are endemic among heterosexuals, too. Religiously inspired lawmakers have also attempted to control the bedroom behavior of heterosexuals, but the "unnatural" argument no longer works effectively for this purpose. It would, say its opponents, require a divine revelation to state what is and what is not natural. The religious right would presume that they themselves are equipped with such a revelation, but many disagree with them, explaining that civilization itself, with its mass transportation, varieties of clothing, and other amenities, is highly unnatural. Must we, therefore, go around naked? Because an individual does not desire certain consensual and harmless behavior himself gives him no good reason to condemn it in others, and yet this is precisely the kind of occupation in which religious fundamentalists are involved. Not only are they self-centered, thinking that what they deny must be denied by all, but they would deny humanity its right to variety, an essence of its being.

NB

Second, fundamentalists condemn homosexuality by pointing to what is known as "the prairie fire effect"—the belief that if there is no taboo homosexuality will engulf the race. This argument is fraught with heterosexual insecurities. Is homosexuality so captivating that no one will be able to resist its charms? To say so is to contradict the previous assumption, that it is unnatural. It is to admit that the homosexual component lies deep in every person, and is therefore one of nature's major inducements. In any case, it is clear that even with as much condemnation as has taken place, the sexual majority has not been able to eliminate homosexuality at all.

Third, arousing fears about the protection of youth has always been a major staple of anti-homosexualism, especially as it is preached today. It is now clear, however, to all but the most benighted observer, that heterosexual males pose the primary threat of sexual abuse against minors. A year-long study conducted by Children's Hospital in Denver, Colorado, revealed that between July 1, 1991, and June 30, 1992, only one out of 387 cases of suspected child molestation was gay-related. Frank Bruni, author of *The Gospel of Shame: Children, Sexual Abuse and the Catholic Church,* says that "men who molest prepubescent boys are most often—by a wide margin—heterosexual in any adult involvements they may have."[8] The protection of youths is relevant to any society, but it has no bearing on same-sex relationships among adults.

Fourth, orthodox religionists contend that homosexuality will lead to race suicide, and that because homosexuals reputedly do not reproduce, their practices will put an end to the human race. This is a particularly unimaginative argument. First, it assumes that there will be no more functioning heterosexuals. Second, it ignores the fact that contraceptives, which fundamentalists also often oppose, can do more than homosexuality to put an end to reproductive behavior and that the world is presently suffering from an overabundance of reproductive behavior.

Fifth, fundamentalists allege that the homosexual is promiscuous and that he gives himself up to perverse sexual practices. This argument can be turned against heterosexuals, too, merely by quoting statistics on unmarried birth rates, or by counting X-rated video sales. Odd sexual practices are, as any sophisticate knows, as common among heterosexuals, but the discovery and cynical use of such practices—such as *analingus* (licking the anus) or *urolagnia* (drinking urine)—provides, for the ignorant, a bogus fundamentalist brush with which to tar homosexuals alone. The fact that gay meeting places have often been relegated to marginal areas of major cities allows religious fanatics to criticize their sordidness. A peculiar twist of logic occurs in that the fanatics push the gay minority into the dark corners of society and then critiques it for being there. When it emerges, sometimes with fanfare, the minority is accused of "flaunting," by which is meant any display of same-sex affection. The Christian Coalition's request to Congress for a bill opposing same-sex marriages shows how fundamentalists hypocritically seek legal denials of loving gay and lesbian relationships while condemning all homosexuals for reputed promiscuity.

The final argument used to deprecate gay men and lesbians is that they are flouting God's laws, especially those in Leviticus demanding the death penalty which were later given updated authority by St. Paul (Rom. 1:26–27). Same-sex lovers, say fundamentalists, are making a mockery of religion. If God's laws are interpreted by Pauline fundamentalist "logic," then this is undeniably so. Thomas Jefferson, however, noted in his biblical studies that "Paul was the great Coryphaeus, and first corrupter of the doctrines of Jesus." Even so, many denominations are trying, painfully, and in spite of St. Paul's oblique commentaries, to come to grips with the realities of homosexuals in their midst. Some in the Protestant tradition accomplish this with more finesse than others, including the Unitarian-Universalists, the Society of Friends (Quakers), certain wings of the Episcopalian church, and the United Church of Christ, all of whom welcome openly gay membership.

▼ ▼ ▼

A foremost producer of anti-gay programming is the long-time ally of the Reverend Jerry Falwell, televangelist D. James Kennedy, pastor of the Coral Ridge Presbyterian Church (Ft. Lauderdale, Florida). Kennedy's tax-exempt hate campaign under his umbrella organization, The Coral Ridge Ministries, has become a constant on numerous stations. He has regularly offered (for $25 or more) a video about the "gay agenda," a blatant propaganda film replete with paranoid visions of a gay/lesbian takeover.

Hostility erupts when gay activists watch Kennedy's falsifying images. Some feel outraged at the disingenuous lies so clumsily manufactured by this Presbyterian man of God. Scotland, which is often regarded as a cradle of Presbyterian doctrine, has, nevertheless, produced Robert Burns, whose poetry poked fun at this very doctrine. Burns' "Holy Willie's Prayer" satirizes the way in which the lustful Presbyterian prays forgiveness for transgressing with a ladyfriend, Meg. He addresses God thusly:

> *But yet O'Lord confess I must*
> *At times I'm fash'd wi' fleshly lust;*
> *An' sometimes, too, with wardly trust,*
> > *Vile self gets in;*
> *But thou remembers we are dust*
> > *Defiled wi' sin.*

> *O Lord! yestreen Thou kens, wi' Meg—*
> *Thy pardon I sincerely beg—*
> *O, may't ne'er be a living plague*
> > *To my dishonor!*
> *An' I'll ne'er lift a lawless leg*
> > *Again upon her.*

Over two hundred years ago, Burns also laughed at dogmas like eternal torment, original sin, and the like. Another segment of "Holy Willie's Prayer" says:

> *What was I, or my generation*
> *That I should get sic exaltation?*
> *I, wha deserv'd most just damnation*
>   *For broken laws*
> *Sax thousand years ere my creation,*
>   *Thro' Adam's cause!*

> *When from my mither's womb I fell,*
> *Thou might hae plung'd me deep in hell*
> *To knash my gooms, and weep, and wail*
>   *In burning lakes,*
> *Where damned devils roar and yell,*
>   *Chained up to stakes.*

> *Yet I am here, a chosen sample,*
> *To show Thy grace is great and ample:*
> *I'm here a pillar of Thy temple,*
>   *Strong as a rock*
> *A guide, a buckler, and example*
>   *To a' Thy flock!* [9]

It may help, when D. James Kennedy preaches, to identify him with Holy Willie. Kennedy, narrating his deceptive video on the "gay agenda," requires more sex, lies, and videotape.

"THE GAY AGENDA *DEMANDS* REPEAL OF ALL SODOMY LAWS AND LEGALIZES ALL FORMS OF SEXUAL EXPRESSION. IT ALSO CALLS FOR LOWERING THE AGE OF CONSENT TO ALLOW SEX WITH YOUTH."

Two-thirds of this statement is patently false. The gay community does seek the repeal of sodomy laws, but only to assure equality with heterosexuals. Such laws, which also affect heterosexual lovers, have already been eliminated in half of the states. Legalizing "all forms of sexual expression," however, without any qualifications is not on the agenda of the gay liberation movement. No major movement strategist worth his salt would be so naive as to make such a proposal. But the Reverend D. James Kennedy is setting off psychological alarms to agitate the repressed and the sexually frustrated with talk of legalizing all forms of sex. This frustration is his bread and butter.

No reputable gay or lesbian organization asks, on sexual grounds, anything more than equality with heterosexuals. When Reverend Kennedy alleges that the gay and lesbian liberation movement hopes to lower age of consent laws to allow sex with youth, this is merely the long-lived anti-gay staple, provoking concern about the protection of youth. Age of consent has never been on any national agenda. It is established by local communities, and drops to as low as sixteen in Washington, D.C. There are organizations for pedophiles, straight or gay (like NAMBLA, the North American Man-Boy Love Association, shown marching behind its banner), but pedophilia is not a gay and lesbian liberation issue. It is an age-of-consent issue and has no bearing on what consenting adults do in private.

"THE GAY AGENDA *DEMANDS* THE DIVERTING OF MASSIVE DEFENSE BUDGET FUNDS TO COVER AIDS PATIENTS' MEDICAL EXPENSES AND IT WOULD ALSO REQUIRE TAXPAYER FUNDING OF SEX CHANGE OPERATIONS."

Lobbyists of every stripe suggested that the end of the cold war meant releasing money, "the peace dividend," for other government uses. Kennedy would link all AIDS groups with gay men. Many such groups, including patient care or disease-research lobbies, seek the diverting of funds from *any* government agencies where they are needlessly squandered so that they can be put into their own more urgent, life-preserving causes. The Reverend Kennedy's propaganda machine deliberately highlights the U.S. defense budget to rile macho right-wing militarists. Kennedy links his gay bashing with legitimate AIDS concerns, in order to persuade his listeners. In doing this he causes harm to the many heterosexual AIDS patients, young and old, whom he lumps with his hated gays, purposefully marginalizing everybody with AIDS, no matter what their orientation. He lacks consideration for babies born into this nightmare disease. To make his point Kennedy would tamper with government funding that works in the best interest of these children, too. Using his brand of "logic," one might say that Kennedy helps pave the way for the maltreatment of AIDS babies.

And would responsible leaders in the gay movement ask taxpayer funding for transsexual operations? Not, I dare say, in the present climate of opinion about taxes. Kennedy's odd claim belongs to larger debates about gender and state medical rationing. Transsexuals, starting with the late Christine Jorgensen, almost always loudly insist that they are not homosexuals. Their cause is their own. It has no easily demonstrable connection with equalizing the civil rights of gay men, bisexuals, and lesbians, who, like heterosexuals, have no wish for cosmetic gender rearrangements.

(*Left*) The author in 1962.

(*Below*) The author, followed by Dr. Franklin E. Kameny and Lilli Vincenz, during a demonstration in front of the White House organized by the Mattachine Society of Washington, D.C., in 1965. Photo courtesy Bettmann Archive.

(*Left*) Barbara Gittings, the pioneering militant activist editor of the first lesbian movement magazine, *The Ladder*, with the author in Philadelphia as they celebrate July 4, 1965, following the first demonstration by the gay and lesbian movement at Independence Hall. Photo by Perrin Shaffer.

(*Below*) The author shown in 1975 with Dr. Franklin E. Kameny, co-founder with the author of the Mattachine Society of Washington. Photo by Ted Richards.

(*Above*) A 1977 photo showing (left) several groups supporting gay and lesbian rights as they protest the appearance of Anita Bryant (right) at a "rally for decency" in Indianapolis. Courtesy AP/Wide World.

(*Right*) The author shown marching with his longtime comrade and lover Lige Clarke at New York's Gay Pride March, 1972. Photo by Lew Williams.

(*Above*) A Columbia University Gay and Lesbian Unity Rally in 1971 showing (left to right): Lige Clarke; the author; New York Gay Activists Alliance (GAA) president/co-founder, Jim Owles; and fellow GAA co-founder, Marty Robinson. Photo by Kay Tobin Lahusen.

(*Left*) Lige Clarke in Greenwich Village, 1969. In 1975 this pioneering author, journalist, and activist was mysteriously murdered in a hail of automatic gunfire at a road block near Vera Cruz, Mexico. Author's files.

The Great Gay and Lesbian March on Washington, D.C., October 11, 1987. Shown (left to right): Perrin Shaffer, one of the first ten marchers in the 1965 White House demonstration; the author; Shelbianna Rhein, sister of the late Lige Clarke; her son, New York artist Eric Rhein; Sandy Zerbe; and an unidentified marcher. Photo by Willis Bivins.

Televangelist Jerry Falwell applauds President Ronald Reagan after introducing him to speak before the Conservative Political Action Conference in Washington, D.C., in 1987. Photo courtesy AP/Wide World.

(*Left*) The Ku Klux Klan shown picketing a gay bar on Merritt Island, Florida, on December 11, 1994. Photo by Steve Yates.

(*Below*) Vice-President Dan Quayle greets televangelist Pat Robertson at the Christian Coalition's "God and Country" rally in Houston in August 1992. Quayle was struggling to overcome his negative poll ratings by emphasizing his belief in "traditional values." Photo courtesy AP/Wide World.

Anti-choice leader Randall Terry (left) looks up as he yells "Hallelujah!" after being given a check for $10,000 by Jerry Falwell (behind microphone). This was during a demonstration outside the Women's Health Center in Atlanta in August 1988. Photo courtesy AP/Wide World.

Saviz Shafaie, pioneering Iranian gay and men's movement activist, shown carrying the rainbow flag at an Orlando, Florida, parade honoring Dr. Martin Luther King, Jr., January 1995. Photo by James Ford.

(*Above*) Christian Coalition Executive Director Ralph Reed talks to Republican presidential hopeful Senator Phil Gramm (R-Texas) during a Capitol Hill news conference, May 1995, to discuss the coalition's "Contract with the American Family." Courtesy AP/Wide World.

(*Left*) Pat Robertson holds hands with PLO chief Yasir Arafat following their meeting in Gaza City in September 1995. Photo courtesy AP/Wide World.

"THE GAY AGENDA REQUIRES CONGRESS TO LEGALIZE ALL SAME-SEX MARRIAGES, AS WELL AS LEGALIZE ADOPTION, CUSTODY, AND FOSTER CARE FOR SO-CALLED HOMOSEXUAL FAMILIES."

Anyone familiar with the art of the possible knows that other steps toward equality must first be made. These matters are addressed in state courts and local municipalities. The Hawaii state legislature, for example, is presently considering marriage rights for same-sex couples, but this is a local matter and no petitions to Congress have been made with respect to gay marriages other than the purposely inflammatory anti-gay-marriage bill favored by the Christian Coalition. As previously mentioned, many gay men and lesbians already celebrate what gay Christian churches call "holy unions." At present, in spite of the fact that half the states have eliminated anti-sodomy laws, no such unions are state-recognized. Except in the very few where domestic partnerships exist, there is no legal recourse for longtime companions who wish to visit their mates in hospitals, no reliable method to ensure the passing of one's estate to a lover at death, no sharing (as exists for heterosexual couples) of health-care insurance benefits, no tax breaks given to same-sex couples such as are given to those of opposite sexes, and no assurance that a gay father or mother (who has children from a previous heterosexual marriage) has legal rights to keep those children. Gay male and lesbian couples have been denied the right to adopt even babies afflicted with AIDS, though few others will take them. The reason lies in the fear, kept banked and burning by fundamentalist fanatics, that such children are at risk for gay molestation, another milking of their "youth protection" theme. At present I know of *no attempt by major gay organizations* to petition Congress for the right to either marry or adopt. On a case-by-case basis gay couples have won or lost adoption rights in various states. A young mother who took a lesbian partner was recently deprived by a Virginia court of her right to keep her own baby, though on appeal to Virginia's Supreme Court, her child was returned to her.

"THE GAY AGENDA REQUIRES THE FULL INCLUSION OF LESBIANS, BISEXUALS, AND TRANSGENDERS IN EDUCATION, CHILD-CARE, AND COUNSELING PROGRAMS."

From within their closets gay men and lesbians have long been part of the educational system, working as teachers and counselors. Fundamentalists denying them the right to be known by school officials as gay, are simply putting another twist on their "youth protection" tirades, hoping to incite parental concern over what is nothing more than an equal employment issue. Students, contrary to the fundamentalists' contrived worry, are more certifiably safe if a gay teacher is known as such by his or her superiors than if he or she is living a secret or closeted life. In Washington, D.C., and elsewhere openly homosexual public school teachers have long enjoyed job protection with no ill effects. Pioneering gay rights advocates carried protest signs as early as 1970 asking "Was Socrates a Lousy Teacher?" In 1994 Academy Award-winning actor Tom Hanks publicly thanked his gay high school teacher who had helped much, he said, to inspire him early in life.

"THE GAY AGENDA REQUIRES CONTRACEPTIVES AND UNRESTRICTED ABORTION SERVICES TO BE MADE AVAILABLE TO ALL PEOPLE REGARDLESS OF AGE."

If the previous claim has been circulated by Reverend Kennedy without his blushing, surely this accusation should elicit from him at least some mild embarrassment. Its intent is clear. The Reverend Kennedy knows that his flock has already rallied against contraceptives and free choice. He sees he can incite the indignation of his followers by connecting gays, condoms, and abortion. Planned parenthood, AIDS activists (gay and straight), and many others favor condom distribution to prevent the yearly U.S. crop of a million unwanted teen pregnancies and to protect citizens from deadly sexually transmitted diseases, but unrestricted condom distribution is *not* on the national gay movement agenda. As for the free choice movement, it is much favored by thinking homosexuals; but gays, like straights, stand on both sides of the abortion issue. Still, as a platform plank, it stands outside the major aims of gay and lesbian liberation itself, though many gay men and lesbians lend their talents to defending the pro-choice position. I wholeheartedly support contraceptives and free choice, not as a gay man but as an individual who sees their import for society generally.

"THE GAY AGENDA REQUIRES AN END TO ALL FORMS OF DISCRIMINATION AND TAX PAYER FUNDING FOR ARTIFICIAL INSEMINATION OF LESBIANS AND BISEXUALS, AND FORBIDS RELIGIOUS-BASED CONCERNS REGARDING HOMOSEXUALITY FROM BEING EXPRESSED."

Again, the Reverend Kennedy tars with too wide a brush. "All forms of discrimination?" What is he talking about? And tax funds to impregnate lesbians? Please. I leave the reader to ask any American lesbian if that is what she wants. The very idea of such a demand, as part of the national movement's agenda, is a bad joke. As for forbidding religious groups from preaching hate in the name of religion, no legal steps against fundamentalists have been taken by the gay and lesbian movement on this question. Some may surely favor FCC rules forbidding such hate mongering on the airwaves, protecting gay communities as is already done in behalf of other minorities. This does not prevent free speech within fundamentalist assemblies; however, their public speech should be monitored, as it is with other hate groups.

"THE GAY AGENDA REQUIRES ORGANIZATIONS SUCH AS THE BOY SCOUTS OF AMERICA TO ACCEPT HOMOSEXUAL SCOUTMASTERS. SO . . . IF HOMOSEXUALS HAVE THEIR WAY THIS WOULD BE QUITE A DIFFERENT AMERICA."

Once again Reverend Kennedy incites fear for youth safety, with no regard for the safety of gay and lesbian teens. In fact, as there have always been gay teachers, there have always been homosexual scoutmasters. The Scouts, however, claim to be a private organization and reject not only openly gay men but the membership of children who do not accept its religious viewpoints. The issue involves community support and United Way funds collected to uphold such anti-American bigotry, and is, like education, one of equal employment opportunity. Driving homosexual scoutmasters into the closet, as in the case with educators, leaves the scouting field open only to one who lives a secretive life, a behavior that can be more worrisome than one that is unembarrassed about sexual preference and therefore less damagingly repressed.

▼ ▼ ▼

The Reverend Kennedy's video, following the listing of the above falsehoods, zooms in on a passionate gay rights speaker, Duke Comegys, a Chair of the Human Rights Campaign Fund, and uses Comegys' oratory *out of context* to indicate support of Kennedy's manufactured gay agenda. Comedes, shouting to a large crowd, says: "And make no mistake about it. We will not stop until we have achieved our freedom, our justice, and our pursuit of happiness." This misuse of Mr. Comedes' speech shows to what lengths the unscrupulous Reverend Kennedy and his allies are willing to stretch the truth.

Kennedy's own voice then narrates: "Homosexuals have gained massive political clout as they seek special protective minority status. Just down the street (on Pennsylvania Avenue) they have more friends." (A photo is shown of Clinton's White House.) "For the first time in history a [Democratic] administration has openly embraced homosexuals and their agenda."

A mock logo of the *Washington Post* (sans date, byline, or readable text) is shown, under which appears the Kennedy-created headline: "Gays Mobilizing for Clinton as Rights Become an Issue." President Clinton is then shown campaigning, telling homosexuals in Los Angeles that gay men and lesbians form "part of my vision for America." The camera cuts to scantily clad male youths dancing together in a disco, followed by a closeup of males kissing. Kennedy continues his narrative:

> Most Americans have never seen or heard what you have witnessed today. But the truth about the homosexual agenda *must* be told. That's why I want to broadcast this program on prime-time television all around the nation. If Americans know the truth we *can* win this battle. Will you help me in this challenge by sending whatever gift you can today? Every gift is vitally important but if you can send $25 or more. I want to thank you by sending you a videocassette copy of this program to share with those in your family or friends.

The approach taken by Kennedy is mild compared to many of his fiery televangelist peers. In various ways they have all echoed Jerry Falwell's contention that "AIDS is God's judgment against homosexuals,"[10] or Pope John Paul II who, when asked by reporters if this was so, replied, "It is not easy to know the intentions of God," while on the same day the Vatican's newspaper asserted that AIDS is "a kind of sanction by Nature." The self-aggrandizing clergymen who make such statements are, in fact, worse than the average witchdoctor.

▼ ▼ ▼

In a nation where sexual ignorance is kept widespread, fundamentalist preachers can still con their audiences with observations about gay men and lesbians that none may question. "I have never seen a homosexual come from a home where both the mother and the father were incurably in love with Jesus Christ and with each other," said Dr. Howard Hendricks, chairman of the Center for Christian Leadership, Dallas Theological Seminary. "Many homosexuals adopted their lifestyle because they were either recruited or seduced as teenagers or pre-teens," writes John Neider, author of *God, Sex & Your Child.*[11] Melvin Anchell, in an interview in the *New American,* says: "When society does not disavow such perversity, but instead begins to glorify these people and their sexual vulgarity, their ranks grow. . . . Where there is no stigma attached to homosexual activity, homosexuals form a large part of the population."[12] These statements have been tailored to provoke alarm. Dr. Hendricks would be laughed out of any reputable researcher's presence. Neider, who pretends expertise on sex, wears his ignorance as a charm. Mr. Anchell, without realizing it, credits homosexuality with better than box-office drawing power. So shocked is he by tales of its very presence that he sees it behind every lamppost and every bush.

As orthodox apologists these know-nothings mouth platitudes about their love for homosexual sinners, insisting they hate not the individuals but the "sin" of homosexual behavior. But they cannot distinguish, in practice, between the celibate but homosexually inclined person and the one who behaves homosexually. Even the gay convert to their nonsense who has declared himself or herself chaste or an "ex-gay," is under extreme suspicion. First, such a person is automatically thought to be an AIDS carrier. Next, it is highly unlikely he or she would be trusted to lead children on walks in the woods during a Sunday School picnic. In *MOODY*, a publication of the Chicago-based Moody Bible Institute, Mona Riley is quoted as seeing "a hardness in the heart of the American church" toward people who have reportedly once been homosexually inclined. "We need to be trained in compassion," she says. "We have judged this sin to be worse than every other, but I don't see that in the Scriptures." In the same magazine Bob Davies says that "ministries around the country recognize hidden barriers that prevent churches from embracing those struggling with homosexuality."[13] Thus homosexuals and "ex-homosexuals" are treated, even if with compassion, in the holy sanctuaries of the Bible Belt as if they had a condition not unlike leprosy.

Today's "religious" hate mongers tell us that homosexuality causes the downfall of civilizations. This quaint rumor, unsubstantiated by any scholar of note, hardly needs a reply. The uplifting contributions of homosexuals to civilizations, past and present, cannot be taken lightly. The Greek city-states died because of the Athenians' military adventurism, greed, economic shortsightedness, and a decay of their resources, not because of the sexual practices which had always characterized their society. In their attempt to marginalize gay men and lesbians, much as Hitler was able to do with Jews, the religious right tells us that the number of gays is insignificant.

Why then do they bother to launch such attacks? And if our numbers are only—as they often say—1 percent of the population, how then can we bring about the downfall of America? But homosexuals number many more than a single percentage point. If same-sex lovers comprise only 1 percent, then well over half of all gay men and lesbians were in Washington, D.C., in 1993 and New York in 1994, when upwards of a million marched at each event. In fact, only a small fraction of America's homosexually inclined masses attend such marches.

The first militant/activist gay and lesbian organization in America was The Mattachine Society of Washington, founded in 1961. In 1964 this Washington group sent a thousand letters to clergy of all faiths in the Washington, D.C., area, asking that they participate in the opening of an historic dialogue with gay men and lesbians. In all, the society received forty replies, ten of which showed willingness to talk. Among the remaining, more negative responses was one from Dr. Frederick Brown Harris, an old school Methodist who was also chaplain of the United States Senate. Reverend Harris, unfortunately, had no knowledge of zoology when he replied to activists in his weekly column published in the *Sunday Star*:

> The attempt to disregard the *you* in you is illustrated in the present propaganda, even over television and radio, to stop even in decent society what is called discrimination of sex deviates and perverts who are addicted to disgusting practices which are not only degrading to those guilty, but whose abnormal debaucheries so often blight the lives of youth lured as sacrifices to such degenerate lust. Such people, we are blandly told, comprise a large minority of the total population.
>
> The present propaganda regarding this nauseating matter is not to rehabilitate these moral lepers, but to integrate them, to accept them without question with practices of

which the lower animals are never guilty. Those who advocate such an attitude seem more concerned with discrimination than with contamination.[14]

The Senate chaplain's tirade was only an early shoot in that vast forest of rampant ignorance and pathological disturbances that would grow in the 1980s to "maturity" as the religious right's crusade against gay men and lesbians got under way. Is it not clear, after reading this minister's words, that conventional "religious" zealots can have no remorse about the host of anti-gay fires they themselves have set and which now burn brightly on every American hilltop?

In the next chapter I examine the "family values" crisis, and how orthodoxy's stress on monogamy and exclusivity not only stigmatizes gay and lesbian relationships, but also works against the full flowering of human potential.

NOTES

1. Leigh W. Rutledge, *Unnatural Quotations* (Boston: Alyson Publications, 1988), p. 42.

2. "Desecrating Yad Vashem," *Jerusalem Post,* June 1, 1994, p. 6.

3. Heinrich Himmer's February 18, 1937, speech to the officer's corps of Hitler's storm troopers, quoted in Mel White, *Stranger at the Gate: To Be Gay and Christian in America* (New York: Simon and Schuster, 1994), p. 225.

4. Ibid.

5. John E. Yang, *Washington Post,* June 13, 1996, p. A–8.

6. Nathan Glazer and David Riesman, *The Intellectuals and the Discontented Classes,* 1955.

7. Nathan Callahan and William Payton, eds., foreword by Oliver Stone, *"Shut Up Fag!": Quotations from the Files of Congressman Bob Dornan, The Man Who Would Be President* (Irvine, Calif.: Mainstreet Media, 1994), p. 53.

8. Eric Marcus, *Is It A Choice?* (San Francisco: HarperCollins, 1993), p. 14.

9. Robert Burns, *Poems and Songs of Robert Burns,* ed. James Barke (London and Glasgow: Collins, 1953), p. 222.

10. David Scruggs, "Falwell Says Bakker Must Not Return," *Orlando Sentinel,* March 26, 1987, p. A–1.

11. John Neider, *God, Sex & Your Child* (Nashville, Tenn.: Thomas Nelson, Inc., 1988), p. 175.

12. Melvin Anchell, interview with John F. McManus, "Unsafe in Any Grade," *The New American,* May 11, 1987.

13. Bon Davies, "Will We Offer Hope?" *MOODY* magazine, May 1994, p. 12.

14. Frederick Brown Harris, "About the You in You," *Sunday Star,* 1964. Quoted in Lige Clarke and Jack Nichols, *I Have More Fun with You Than Anybody* (New York: St. Martin's Press, 1972), p. 132.

The Family Values Crisis

Your children are not your children.
They are the sons and daughters of Life's longing for itself.
They come through you but not from you,
And though they are with you yet they belong not to you.

Kahlil Gibran[1]

FUNDAMENTALISM OR ORTHODOXY, no matter the denominational guise, banks its hopes for longevity on an old "sacred" word, family. Fashioning fervent appeals for the restoration of its own "proper" interpretation of this word, it calls its sales gimmick *Family Values*.

Fundamentalist preachers have wrapped themselves simple-mindedly in the family values flag, blaming feminist theories and the sexual revolution of the 1960s, purposely ignoring the fact that present-day economic necessities require both parents to work. These orthodox nostalgians and others trumpet the "need" for a return to an imaginary perfect past and advise that women, if possible, should stay at home and care for their young. With rising costs, diminishing salaries, corporate downsizing, and population growth, most American mothers can ill afford such a luxury. There are many successful *single* parents who do not fit into the fundamentalist *Family Values* straitjacket.

Many Americans, no matter what their orientation, live in "family" arrangements that do not suit dogmatic religionists. Those who preach the fundamentalist agenda make vain attempts to crush any definitions of *family* that stand outside a narrow sectarian focus. Nuclear family units comprised of authoritative father-providers, obedient domestic-mothers, and appropriately indoctrinated children are, in their view, to be embraced as the norm. Not only gay men and lesbians, but single parents, working mothers, and secular child-care facilities are subjected, on this fundamentalist-orthodox agenda, to intense criticism.

In reply, let it be clear that little is usually said by fundamentalists about these nuclear family arrangements which isn't supportive of conservative ideals, conformist, and, unfortunately, suffering severely from a much too schmaltzy sentimentalism. No, the nuclear family is not ailing because of assaults by feminist or gay propagandists. Changes are taking place because of profound social antecedents to which feminism, in its many guises, has merely posited polemical responses. A growing body of women's literature and women's studies provides abundant historic evidence of major struggles against an ascendant patriarchal value system. Among the major causes of today's social revolutions is woman's entry into the economic sphere in the twentieth century.

Other factors foster extreme social disarray, including fundamentalist male values like male dominance that lead to spousal and child abuse, domestic violence, and even patricide or matricide. Brutal examples of nuclear family dysfunction are daily news, yet fundamentalism and orthodoxy offer nothing more to social discourse than unlikely mass conversions to specific supernatural beliefs that will supposedly cure the alienation and disintegration routinely suffered by those bound together in "holy" ties. Indeed, what stands *most* in the way of better human bonding are orthodox/fundamentalist rules that lead to a restrictive, suffocating concept of family. These "religious" rules impede a maximization of affection, keeping it tightly corralled, usually through legal locks certifying a first step into long-term bondage. The current commercial culture, too, which is caused by market forces, co-opts gays as often as straights. Young lesbians who thumb through mainstream magazines featuring photos of bridal gowns, or gay men who seek stability through legal rituals and meaningful signatures on paper, are just as much dupes of cultural standards as are their straight counterparts. As a result of such programming there are large numbers of gay men and lesbians who seek nuclear family units of their own. My personal agenda contains no structuring for such familial units, whether gay or straight. "One's self I sing," says the first line in Walt Whitman's *Leaves of Grass,* "a simple separate person." Yet the good gay poet strove emotionally to understand all humankind as his extended family.

Ritualized aspects of American culture have followed routinely upon the heels of centuries-old but now absurd religious definitions. The larger society must now reassess these definitions, which turn spouses into each other's wardens who come and go only as allowed by the other. Some have taken to carrying beepers or telephones as a means of constant contact. They socialize only with those who are like themselves. There is a dual understanding of what makes for acceptable conversations in the home and moronic restrictions on basic behaviors, covering not only physical postures but the limits of thought processes as well. Unit members are supposed to be happy campers though they have been regulated in every significant movement they make. Intense sexual guilt is instilled by orthodox/fundamentalist lecturing. The uncritical believer fears for his own ability to self-govern in sexual matters and, because he does not self-trust, he impugns others as "animals" in his pitiful bid to erase the sorry consciousness of his own sexual repression. Instead of turning his moral focus toward himself or genuine world-saving causes, he turns instead, armed with bitter hatreds, to scapegoating.

The fundamentalist program for heterosexual bonding is on the table for all to see. Let me bring as much clarity to my examination as possible. But beforehand, let there be positive statements about close bonding. I say: encourage bonding without bonds, just as does the mystic poet Kahlil Gibran in his discourse on marriage in his famed book *The Prophet*:

> *Love one another, but make not a bond of love:*
> *Let it rather be a moving sea between the shores of your souls.*
> *Fill each other's cup but drink not from one cup.*
> *Give one another of your bread but eat not from the same loaf.*
> *Sing and dance together and be joyous, but let each one*
> *of you be alone,*
> *Even as the strings of a lute are alone though they quiver*
> *with the same music.*[2]

In bonding, people can best assist each other by remaining financially and emotionally self-contained. I look forward to a society structured primarily for individuals rather than for coupled or nuclear-unit survival. Each person, in this arrangement attains the dignity of a unit.

Nigel Nicolson's *Portrait of a Marriage*, a book praised by the late Max Lerner, is a son's description of his parent's *triumphant* marriage which, in spite of the fact that both had extramarital affairs, including bisexual ones, enjoyed the raising of two sons, intimate friends, and a well-ordered castle surrounded by gardens they tended together. The son-chronicler praises their *comradeship,* the Whitmanesque word for close affectionate bondings. Lerner suggests that "in some ways it was a marriage of true minds, and they did not admit into it the impediments that would have destroyed it." He continues: "We have learned that marriage can have a variety of sexual and affectional bases, with shared ties that give both people the continuities all of us need."[3]

Only by disconnecting finances from affection can a more genuine affection between two or more grow. The orthodox system, because it ties lovemaking to a patriarch's support money, often leads to an unscrupulous manipulation by women and thoughtless domination by men. These behaviors militate against honesty. They lead, in the midst of nuclear "family" units, to loneliness, and, along the way, to boredom and frustration as marital functioning ceases to provide a healthy psychological lifeline. Speaking critically of conventional marriage, the acclaimed French intellectual and feminist Simone de Beauvoir described it as "a very alienating institution, for men as well as for women. . . . It's a very dangerous institution, dangerous for men who find themselves trapped, saddled with a wife and children to support; dangerous for women, who aren't financially independent and end up depending on men who can throw them out when they are forty; and dangerous for children because their parents vent all their frustrations on them."[4]

None but the narrowest approach to love would insist, as fundamentalists and their ilk do, that monogamy is its only virtuous, fulfilling, and loving expression. Clearly, fundamentalists enforce their obligatory practice and form thereby a primary obstacle to the maximization of affection. The fundamentalist code, as long as it deprives mature adults of their full consensual freedom to touch others, whether in erotic or Platonic affection, robs its converts of their full humanity. Any altruistic feelings they may have get blocked by egocentric insecurities (the "harem complexes") refusing their mates outside contacts. The religious right thereby deprives its adherents of the very essence of personal freedom: the right after marriage of an individual to decide to whom, among any and all, the benefits of his or her affection should go. What kind of relationships evolve under this closed system? Those in which intimacy is so fragile that it cannot suffer the loved one's generous impulses toward others. Any mate who flies into a jealous rage reveals sad truths about his or her relationship, namely, that he or she has little knowledge of a spouse, little trust, little rapport, all betraying an insecure and selfish conviction that attraction must be regulated to allow marrieds their delusions of *possession*. Fidelity is thus reduced by a sexual tunnel vision that ignores truly significant expressions of loyalty. This says little for the value placed by a jealous individual on important nonsexual qualities, those that create useful harmonies in individual lives. The orthodox/fundamentalist take on marriage enthrones and blesses specific *expectations* and demands that insidiously work against many kinds of natural intimacy.

An objection often raised is: "But what if the jealous person loves too much?" Brad Pitt replied to this question somewhat philosophically when playing the title character in the film *Johnny Suede*. He said: "It is the open hand that holds on tightest." And is it not true that modern gay men and lesbians approach same-sex romance with many of the same expectations held by heterosexuals? Are they not jealous in possibly the same proportion? Yes, because gay men and lesbians, like their straight counterparts, are much influenced by traditional mores and also by the current ideas of what constitutes romantic success in their given environments.

Even so, jealousy also shows that a man or woman fears facing the self as a unit. This neurotic malfunction has its basis in cultures that rear children to develop an emotionally dependent status rather than one that is self-regulating and autonomous. Fundamentalist or orthodox married couples diminish their ability to see how they relate to a larger world because, as sequestered mates, they lack important enriching or validating experiences with those outside their units.

Both men and women are forced under fundamentalism into second-class citizenship unless they marry. Then they are invited to socials composed of other marrieds. Singles of both sexes, are, if invited, often considered threats to the exclusivist units and are made to feel unwelcome if assumed to be "on the prowl." To enjoy society's benefits men and women must swear to forego all other intimate affectionate encounters. If either marital partner seeks a way out of the arrangement through divorce or separation, the social pressures launched by neighbors and acquaintances can be stifling, and the revenge sought by one partner or the other in courts, expensive.

Not surprisingly, statistics about the state of the nuclear family show that children fare better in day care centers than at home. According to a study made by the Family Research Center at the University of New Hampshire, children are twice as safe in day care centers. When Dan Quayle trumpeted the need for fathers in each home, he ignored the findings of the National Committee for the Prevention of Child Abuse, according to which most sexual assaults in the home are the work of fathers or stepfathers. He also ignored the *Journal of the American Medical Association* which said that more women are injured in domestic violence than in car accidents or muggings, and nearly half of those murdered are slain by husbands.[5] "The most dangerous place for women is the home," says Joan Stiles of the Massachusetts Coalition for Battered Women.

Homophobic journalist and presidential hopeful Pat Buchanan bridles at the idea of children suing their parents. Did he forget the father of nine, Herman McMillan, who locked his children away for nine years in one filthy room? Should these abused children be without legal recourse in such a situation? Should those outside a nuclear family unit be unable to interfere when they see parents go overboard with "discipline"? David Berreby, writing in the *New York Times,* says that former President George Bush was silly to say that "parents know best." This statement has no more validity, Berreby explains, than saying "government knows best."[6] When fundamentalists complain of government interference in parental matters, especially in areas like sex education or disallowing public school prayers, they show their own ignorance of the often questionable state of the families to whom they'd give all power. Despite Berreby's complaint, government sometimes does know best. It teaches rainbow curriculums promoting race tolerance, religious variety, and ethnic assimilation. Such far-sighted vision as is shown by many public educators stands head and shoulders over biased boondocks indoctrination in "religious" fundamentalist family units. Demagogues have often used the family hierarchy to instill treacherous political programs. Wilhelm Reich stated in *The Mass Psychology of Fascism* that "the authoritarian state has a representative in every family, the father; in this way he becomes the state's most valuable tool."[7] Hitler, calling himself the führer, the father of his nation, saw individual fathers—linked to his state apparatus by employment—as his emissaries to their related underlings, those wives and offspring who, according to St. Paul, must be "submissive" and "obedient" to him.

▼ ▼ ▼

Fundamentalist parents and others conditioned by macho-cult values at the heart of "religious" gender demands, intrude on the personalities of their children. They give them their affectations; their "original sin brand" of self-esteem; their lack of spontaneity, curiosity, and independence. Fortunately some children escape this cloying fundamentalist suffocation. But others are damaged permanently. Though the fundamentalists claim to stand for family unity, their campaign of hatred against gay men and lesbians is a major cause of family disruption. "The essence of being a boring person," writes Dr. David Cooper, "is not to have gone beyond, in imagination at least, the limited horizons of one's family, and to repeat or collude with repetitions of this restrictive system outside the family. . . . In short, to be a boring person is to be a family person, a person who finds the primacy of her or his existence in the mirror reflection rather than in the mirrored."[8]

Maria Montessori, describing the young children in her care, wrote:

> Above all they sought to render themselves independent of adults in all the actions which they could manage on their own, manifesting clearly the desire not to be helped, except in cases of absolute necessity. And they were seen to be tranquil, absorbed, and concentrating on their work, acquiring a surprising calm and serenity.[9]

The cultural influences on any agenda related to rational childrearing would instill the sort of early independence which the Montessori schooling system has already inculcated in thousands of living exemplars. The liberation of children from the fundamentalist nuclear family arrangement must begin by encouraging in children that autonomy that is rightfully theirs, helping them establish a connection between themselves and a much wider environment than fundamentalism recognizes. The sooner dependent children can be made independent, the more will these young people grow to have self-possession, a characteristic sadly missing in current cultural ideals.

The servility that the fundamentalist father demands—what conservative columnist William Safire hails as the recognition by family members of his *intrinsic* authority[10]—is kept orderly as long as it appears to that father that certain rules are being followed. The most important rule is that a wife must copulate only with him. If he is impotent, she has no other recourse. Masturbation continues to violate orthodox doctrine. If her husband is a clumsy and inadequate lover, she must not complain for fear of cracking his fragile ego. Following rules, unfortunately, does nothing to help a man know either his mate or his children better. Since male and female roles remain destructively distinct and separate the interests of the sexes, husbands often put their wives on reserve to satisfy only a portion of their desires. This approach works against marital unity. Patriarchal dominators characteristically lack empathy and an awareness of the feelings of others. The dominator remains satisfied with such an arrangement only while those who *submit* continue to behave in a manner that matches what they *seem* while subservient. Many wives soon grow tired of pretending to be what they are *not* in order to lay claim to dubious rewards.

The time has arrived to reject nostalgia for traditional familial groupings and to seek new ways to realize the satisfaction they once brought. More encompassing definitions of family that bypass blood-line requirements must be instituted. With population exploding unchecked, there is no likelihood that the large family of past centuries will return to favor. Some believe that the downsizing of the nuclear family unit portends its eventual extinction. In recent decades there has been much talk of how ailing elders can no longer count on their offspring to care for them. Now they are sent to nursing homes. But the same overpopulation crisis, as well as the evaporation of economic opportunities once taken for granted, has brought into being a new development.

As it now stands, humankind's best potential has been hijacked by reigning religious sects. The words "father" and "mother" or "husband" and "wife" have been given a sacred status, but one that is deserved only when circumscribed by a much greater word: *friend.* What must be done?

No one, I would wager, has certifiably perfect answers to how humankind can best approach this critical juncture in its development. But it does not seem that basing any such approach on deceptive fundamentalist dogmas will help. At best a careful thinker can do little more than point to specific blocks that obstruct personal integrity and, as a result, stand in the way of more satisfying interpersonal contacts, summoning a differently constructed value system that runs counter to present-day failures. If it is recognized by the majority as sane, it will help create, hopefully, fresh new kinds of relationships, bearing no resemblance to past rituals, but opening doors to greater measures of individual happiness and a resultant sociability now sadly lacking. Gay men and lesbians, too, may wish to reflect on the degree to which they have assimilated old-fashioned approaches to relationships. As author John Rechy puts it, "We're constantly having conservative homosexuals say that we need to get married, to adopt children, join the army. . . . In effect the heterosexual is turned into a parent and we're saying we're nice children, and we're going to be just like you. . . . I don't want that kind of heterosexual shit put on me."[11]

Any life-enhancing agenda must point to the need for a worldwide embrace that celebrates the comradeship of the one with the many. This embrace would reclaim the fundamental goodness of consensual physical contact and maximize affection so that its socially redeeming effects may be claimed by a wider portion of the race. The difference between this approach to love and affection and that of fundamentalist orthodoxies is that this one destroys love's exclusivity by marrying humanity to itself, celebrating self-containment and self-reliance as the best hope for the recreation and replacement of traditional dependencies. This would require an infinite increase in simple tactile expression and in emotionally effusive and affectionate contact among all races and peoples, especially society's isolates, those who are wheelchair-bound or otherwise handicapped and thus too often denied a helping hand extended to foster human sociability. Traditions helping to instill the increase of such contact include the great mystic world-class poets of all times and places, poets who shared a powerful vision of human kinship. Some, like Walt Whitman, were undeniably homosexual by inclination. Others, like Robert Burns, were just as undeniably heterosexually inclined.

Society must work at increasing communal joys that will help replace broken family ties. These joys will evolve not through the reproduction of one's own gene pool, but in the camaraderie that grows among individuals who share values, working together to embody humanity's finer virtues, those which follow on the heels of self-awareness and ignite a genuine compassion for others.

No relationships among these individualists need destroy themselves by bowing before popular cultural idols. Between *comradeship* and fundamentalist coupling, there is a major difference. Comrades allow one another to be themselves, and to come and go at leisure. A comrade looks to him/her self for identity rather than to a dual-partner identification system. He nurturingly encourages others to become themselves rather than to obey his particular system or anybody else's. This, he knows from experience, is love's best gift since self-regulation brings its own undeniable recompense.

Tied in with the orthodox stress on "family values" is the biblical command to "be fruitful and multiply." The next chapter looks at the drastic results of relentless heterosexual supremacy: overpopulation and a declining quality of life for us all.

NOTES

1. Kahlil Gibran, "On Children," *The Prophet* (New York: Alfred A. Knopf, 1923), p. 18.

2. Ibid., "On Marriage," p. 16.

3. Quoted in Jack Nichols, *Men's Liberation: A New Definition of Masculinity* (New York: Penguin, 1975).

4. Simone de Beauvoir, *The Second Sex*, ed. and trans. H. M. Parshley (New York: Alfred A. Knopf, Inc., 1953).

5. David Berreby, "I'm The Anti-Family Voter," *New York Times*, August 29, 1992, section 1, p. 19.

6. Ibid.

7. Wilhelm Reich, *The Mass Psychology of Fascism*, trans. Theodore Wolfe (New York: Orgone Institute, 1946).

8. Dr. David Cooper, *The Death of the Family* (New York: Random House, 1971).

9. Maria Montessori, *Il Bambino in famiglia* (Milan: Gazenti Editore, 1956).

10. William Safire, "What Fathers Want," *New York Times*, June 16, 1994, section A, p. 27.

11. John Rechy, quoted in *Unnatural Quotations*, ed. Leigh W. Rutledge (Boston: Alyson Publications, 1988).

7

Overpopulation and Orthodoxy

Nature appears to be perfectly lavish in the matter, and careless of the waste of seed and of life that may ensue, provided her object of race-propagation is attained; and naturally when the time arrives that Man, objecting to this waste, faces up to the problem, he finds that it is no easy one to solve.

Edward Carpenter[1]

HOMOSEXUALITY, WHETHER MALE or female, is often attacked by orthodox Protestants and Roman Catholics as "barren," and many proffer the "argument" that it would lead to race suicide, since, as they often say, "homosexuals do not reproduce." This is a telling argument which speaks volumes against its fundamentalist proponents and detracts significantly from their alleged reputation for social awareness because of the thoughtless reproductive agenda they promote. While it might be precipitous to suggest homosexuality as a method of birth control, one should not shrink from suggesting that all cultures may wish to consider its joys once the full horror of orthodoxy's thoughtless reproductive agenda has been digested.

Homosexuality is linked with birth control and abortion as the central concerns of any religious organization seizing major social controls through the insidious psychological manipulation of sexual mores. This linking of same-sex love and birth control seems relevant to fundamentalists because both approach sexual expressions as good and proper in themselves, and, therefore, flout orthodox religious dogmas since neither homosexuals nor those who practice birth control have any "high-minded" intentions of reproducing.

In June 1994 Pope John Paul II presided over "an extraordinary gathering" of 114 of his 139 cardinals to voice his opposition to "a pervasive feminist influence" at a forthcoming September United Nations population-growth conference in Cairo. This conference would recommend how governments could best deal with extremes of population growth over the next twenty years. The current global population is estimated at 5.7 billion and could rise to an estimated 10 billion within two decades. Organizers of the Cairo conference would stabilize world population at 7.2 billion by 2050, but the *New York Times* reported that for months the pope had gone to "extraordinary lengths" to oppose United States proposals that recommended the participation of women at the conference.[2] This was because he feared what he considered the undue influence of a feminist presence there. The conference organizers' proposals did not specifically rule out abortion, though they did not recommend it. The *Times* called attention to the deaths of some 250,000 women who perish annually because of unsafe abortions. To oppose the U.S. proposals the pope made a useless personal phone call to President Clinton and personally reprimanded the conference's Pakistani secretary general. In March he sent letters to heads of state "seeking to persuade them that it is not the United Nation's job to lay down moral principals under the guise of population policy."

Why was the pope so concerned? A Vatican official replied thusly, his concerns pointing subliminally to unmarried or nonprocreative sexual behaviors such as birth control and homosexuality: "This conference is very different from previous population conferences. It is basically about a style of libertine, individualistic lifestyle, and it would be the first time the United Nations would endorse this lifestyle."[3]

The 114 cardinals voted unanimously to support battle lines drawn in a speech by John Cardinal O'Connor of New York, who said: "Neither the Cairo conference nor any other forum should lend itself to cultural imperialism or to ideologies that isolate the human person in a self-enclosed universe wherein abortion on demand, sexual promiscuity and distorted notions of the family are proclaimed as human rights or proposed as ideals for the young."[4]

The Roman Church has long opposed "artificial" birth-control methods by calling them incentives to promiscuity. Even the arrival of death-dealing sexually transmitted diseases has failed to soften that opposition. Fundamentalist Protestants link arms with Vatican policy makers on this issue, not only assuring that there will be no distribution of condoms to sexually overactive teens, but refusing, through their influence on many school boards, the right of teachers to mention condoms in sex education classes. County school boards under fundamentalist influences backed the Vatican in this matter just as AIDS was spreading among adolescents.

The response to the AIDS crisis has been criminally sidetracked by the need to stand up to fundamentalist pressures about condoms. Community leaders have been slow to face AIDS as the number one killer of young women (ages 25–29) in New York. And it is not taking smaller towns much time to catch up with this staggering statistic. But with the average time of AIDS incubation (five to ten years), we can look forward to today's youths dying like flies within the next decade. Will prudish religionists send them to their death from AIDS? Will we then think kindly of anti-sex "religious" crusades, as respectable teachers are forbidden to discuss condoms? Or could it be that we will see that decision as one taken by late-twentieth-century primitives who compromised with witch-doctory and perished as a result?

Many began to see the popes as poor men's *witchdoctors* when Pope Paul VI issued his encyclical, *Humanae Vitae* (1968), signing, some said, what was perhaps the death warrant of humanity and making him the worst mass murderer of all time. Paul VI allowed only the *rhythm method,* described best by Catholic critics who called it "Vatican Roulette." This method, as increasing numbers discovered, was a worrisome joke. When sailors on shore leave or traveling salesmen returned to their Catholic spouses, the wives were too often found in the "not right now" phase of their careful calendar markings. But the dance of their hormones won out over the unnatural demands of a papal celibate. Following the publication of *Humanae Vitae,* hundreds of thousands of alienated American Roman Catholics either left the church or defied the pope's ruling. Believers in good standing, who nevertheless used condoms, were excused by many humane priests whose coffers were getting bare and who saw no profit, just because of a little pill, in alienating those regular tithing types. In the intervening years the more open-minded priests of American Catholicism have, in many locales, been pragmatic about sexual matters and have whispered criticisms of the Holy See.*

---

*Many of these priests knew well that nobody was paying attention to the pope in his own Italian back yard. Italy, in 1993, fell lowest on the international scale of births per woman.[5] A mythic image, that of the fertile Italian Mama, her brood surrounding her, proved false even though 97

Until a winning case in 1936 was pressed in a U.S. District Court *against* laws prohibiting physicians to talk of "artificial" birth-control methods, Massachusetts and Connecticut blithely violated free speech guarantees on the subject. In 1937 the American Medical Association publicly endorsed birth control. The personal trials and struggles of pioneer birth-control advocate Margaret Sanger constitute a famous chapter about orthodox religious influences on America. In 1916 she opened the first birth-control clinic in America, in the Brownsville section of Brooklyn. Because of what were believed to be pressures from interfering Roman Catholic clerics, Sanger was indicted and spent thirty days in prison. Her trials offer a telling casebook lesson on how unwarranted tampering in the lives of nonbelievers restricts the free flow of information about sex and reproductive matters.[6]

In the July 1993 issue of his diocesan newspaper, *The Bulletin,* Bishop Norman F. McFarland of Orange County, California, gave his best reasons for supporting the 1968 papal anti-birth-control edict.[7] He wrote, "Welcome to the end of the twentieth century and its revered logo, the condom," as he attempted in his widely circulated missive to lay blame at the

---

percent of all Italians are baptized, married, and buried by the church. The following of certain traditions, however, is no indicator of honest doubts or specific beliefs. Residents of Washington, D.C., for example, report they tend to lend less majesty to the president and his administration. Living in Rome the pope and his Vatican advisors become to Romans their well-known neighbors and are more thought of that way than as God's own representatives. Perhaps familiarity has bred a mild contempt. Italian men no longer show their machismo by siring large families. Moreover, with fewer children, they notice that their wallets are fatter. Meanwhile the Vatican's bankers bemoan a noticeable shrinkage of funds. Condoms, which some AIDS activists have placed in their collection plates, add to that shrinkage.

feet of birth control and the movement for sexual and gender liberation. During "the past thirty years," McFarland laments:

▼ *"Illegitimate births have gone from 5.3 percent to 28 percent."* Bishop McFarland must be informed that a truly humane society would treat the fact of birth, not its church/state sanction, as conferring automatic legitimacy to each living being. And to blame birth control for too many births is, shall we say, odd.

▼ *"Children with single mothers [have gone] from 8 percent to 28.6 percent."* Did birth control cause the unmarried status of these mothers? No. Is the bishop relying on scientific data by placing blame where he does? No. Is the single mother crowd still with this bishop?

▼ *"Children on welfare [range] from 3.5 percent to 12.5 percent."* This number has also been aggravated because birth-control devices were not used.

▼ *"The teenage suicide rate [has gone] from 3.6 percent to 11.3 percent."* Could this be because of unworthy sexual guilt reprehensibly manufactured and encouraged by the bishop's organization in its transparent bid to control young minds at their very cores? And does the bishop take into account that one-third of all teen suicides stem from the increased anti-gay hate mongering of "religious" institutions such as his own?

▼ *"SAT scores have dropped from 975 to 899."* Youthful libertinism is to blame, and condoms? Hardly. Parental negligence, TV hypnotics, a national deficit that precludes "luxuries" like pencils and books as well as the changeover from the literary to the visual in youth culture all have their certain effects. So does a multitude of other possible causes. But birth-control devices? That's stretching it.

▼ *"Violent crimes (per 100,000 people) have risen from 16.1 percent to 75.8 percent."* This statistic sounds somehow askew, Bishop, but okay, blame everything, to get your way, on contraceptives and sexual liberation. Just remember, you and your organization have reportedly been granted the power to cleanse the conscience of even the most rabid murderer. Since you are said to possess such a useful gift, no doubt you're hopeful some percentage of these offenders will seek forgiveness in your confessional booths. Knowing eventually that you'll engineer their quick forgiveness must, in many cases, encourage some rather long-lasting crime sprees. Is it not possible that by thus washing away the weight of sin, your organization has, by downplaying real self-examination, driven a stake into the very heart of meaningful character building?

▼ *"We also have today the highest teen-pregnancy rate in American history."* And still you don't want a word whispered about condoms?

▼ *"The AIDS epidemic."* Listen, dear Bishop, condoms *would* help reduce AIDS, especially in those many poorer countries where your organization, through political maneuvering, interferes with knowledge and distribution of them and where already millions are dying. Would it help to call you a liar? No. As Robert G. Ingersoll, the greatest freethinking orator of the nineteenth century, once put it, "I don't believe in calling a man a liar simply because he's a bishop. It's bad enough to call a man a bishop!"

▼ *"The highest abortion rate in the Western World."* Since the United States has a larger population than any other country in the West, why is this so surprising? According to the Alan Guttmacher Institute, however, 1994 showed a thirteen-year low in performed abortions which, in any case, have been legal only since 1973, throwing a wrench into your aforementioned "thirty-year" format. Are you and your organization, Bishop, planning to house and feed millions of desperately unwanted children to reduce suffering and crime statistics? The lives of children born with AIDS, the plights of cocaine- or alcohol-addicted mothers, and the many addicted children who are born *suffering* you seem not to take into account. Do you know any church "fathers" who will adopt *all* these children? A few to make your dogmas look good. But how many can they take? Not enough.

▼ *"Record child abuse."* If child abuse is your organization's concern, does it plan to adopt and feed 40,000 children dying daily worldwide from malnutrition and starvation? Or would the pope rather agitate politically to prevent the spread of birth-control devices? His answer is clearly on the table. And can we forget that record numbers of Catholic priests have been accused of child molestation?

▼ *"Rape."* Rapists seem, as a rule, not at all concerned about birth-control matters. Don't blame the sexual liberationists for this one. Papal sexual repression leading to ignorance and frustration helps create the resultant violence that impels them.

▼ *"Incest."* This is not new. It's as old as the Bible's very own wino, Lot, and his two enticing daughters (Gen. 19: 31–38).

▼ ▼ ▼

What will happen if religionists have their way in opposing birth control and promoting their narrow definition of "normal" sexuality? Let's take a look at some dreadful scenarios.

Lester Brown, president of the Worldwatch Institute, a prestigious environmental research group, says that food yields are shrinking drastically as populations grow. "The only sensible option may now be an all-out effort to slow population growth," he writes. "The first step is to fill the family planning gap by expanding services. But unless the world can go beyond that and attack the conditions that foster rapid population growth, namely, discrimination against women and widespread poverty, reversing the decline may not be possible."[8] To Mr. Brown's recommendations one might add a much needed full-scale public critique of orthodox "religious" programming and its crusade against nonreproductive sex.

David Pimentel, a Cornell University ecologist, stated in February 1994 that the earth's land, water, and cropland are disappearing so rapidly that global population must be slashed to 2 billion (instead of the present 5.7 billion) by 2100 in order to provide prosperity for all. The alternative, if current trends continue, is a population of 12 billion to 15 billion people and an "apocalyptic worldwide scene of absolute misery, poverty, disease, and starvation."[9]

Poverty among the nation's infants and toddlers is now increasing dramatically, according to the General Accounting Office, the investigative arm of Congress. By 1990, 20 percent of all American infants and toddlers were living in poverty. In many areas, both urban and rural, the percentage climbed as high as 50 percent. Poor children under age three had risen, during the 1980s, by 26 percent from 1.8 million to 2.3 million. If it is true that a civilization's worth can be measured by how it takes care of its weakest inhabitants, the helpless are now, in America and elsewhere in Christendom, without life rafts. A wide-ranging three-year study prepared by the Carnegie Corporation of New York paints "a bleak picture of disintegrating families, persistent poverty, high levels of child abuse, inadequate health care, and child care of such poor quality that it threatens youngsters' intellectual and emotional development."[10]

And yet the religious right continues to concern itself with the rights of the unborn, to inveigh against all forms of non-procreative sex, oblivious of the welfare of children and adults presently alive. In these orthodox "religious" protests against free choice, gays, and birth control, there is a chilling Orwellian factor at work. Wrong becomes a religious right.

In 1992 the National Academy of Sciences and the Royal Society of London issued a report warning: "If current predictions of population growth prove accurate and patterns of human activity on the planet remain unchanged, science and technology may not be able to prevent either irreversible degradation of the environment or continued poverty for much of the world." The ecological damage slated to be caused by the Vatican's monstrous doctrines are not yet widely appreciated, but Latin American areas once green have been ravaged as pitifully poor Catholics have cut down huge forests in search of firewood. At this rate, in another twenty years there will be no forests, and still the popes will marshal their powers to prevent the circulation of condoms and birth-control pills. At the same time, orthodox dogmatists will continue to crowd the planet with know-nothings like themselves, refusing those of us who do not wish to reproduce our right to disconnect baby making from sexual pleasure. No "artificial" protection for us, no RU 486, no onanism, no homosexuality, just millions upon millions of orthodox or fundamentalist believers multiplying ad infinitum, world with an end, amen!

The power of business interests,which honor materialistic ideals promoting a consumer culture and destructive overdevelopment, also must share blame for planetary illnesses with these dogmatic religionists. Emissaries like Charles Colson, who rush between churches and businesses, keep the religious and the commercial empires leaning on one another for support. Both pay homage to the military-industrial complex. The tax-free churches push their own special programs while propagandizing, as do Jerry Falwell, Pat Robertson, and others, the need for a strengthened military machine where most tax revenues continue to be deposited. Meanwhile, all of these institutions threaten human survival. "Without mighty strides in agricultural and medical technology and in political stability, world hunger may emerge as a Malthusian defining issue of the twenty-first century," says author Sam Roberts, nightly New York TV interviewer and urban affairs columnist for the *New York Times.* He explains that "Bangladesh, with a land mass smaller than Wisconsin, could surpass the present population of the United States by 2025. 'Even if by some miracle of science enough food could be produced to feed them,' wrote M.F. Perutz of Cambridge University, 'how could they find the gainful employment needed to buy it?' "[11]

Yale Professor Paul Kennedy, in his book *Preparing for the Twenty-First Century,* explains that overcrowding will not affect poor countries alone. Regional conflicts, global warming, and refugees and their border crossings everywhere will be common occurrences. According to *Earth Journal* (1993), a quarter of a million people are born daily, or 95 million persons per year. In 1995, according to the Population Institute, 100 million were born. Presently (according to Second Harvest, the largest U.S. network of food banks), one in ten American citizens relies on food aid, nearly half of whom are children. Nearly twenty-six million frequent food pantries, soup kitchens, and emergency feeding programs. Bread for the World, the foremost grass-roots Christian anti-hunger organization, stated in its fourth annual hunger report that 30 million Americans go to bed hungry each night, 36.9 million Americans live below the poverty line, and 1.3 billion people across the globe live in absolute poverty.

The Reagan administration, under the influence of the religious right, sabotaged a world population conference held in Mexico City in 1984, by taking what *New York Times* columnist Anthony Lewis called "ironically, the classic Marxist view of population growth," namely, that it is a "neutral" phenomenon. And yet anyone who has traveled to South Asia, Latin America, and Africa knows, says Lewis, "that the pressure of population is taking its toll already, in nature and human psychology." He writes:

> In the cities of China the crowds can be claustrophobic. In the mountains of India and Nepal people desperate for fuel have denuded forests, so topsoil is being washed into rivers and out to sea. . . . Already 20 million Mexicans live in Mexico City, many under appalling conditions. Half the country's people live without sewers, and a quarter without safe water. . . . Rational self-interest, not just humane concern, should make the rich countries do all they can to prevent overpopulation and the suffering and strife it brings.[12]

For centuries fundamentalism and orthodoxy have preached that the world is coming to an end. It seems to me that believers constitute an army of front-line troops working feverishly to bring about what they hope for, and that each one of them assuming a position of political power is but another nail in the planet's coffin. Ronald Reagan's secretary of the interior, James Watt, was also an evangelical who took a prominent seat, following the Jim and Tammy Bakker fiasco, on PTL-TV broadcasts. It was reported that he'd said there's no need to save the planet because the Second Coming of the Lord is imminent.

NOTES

1. Edward Carpenter, "The Intermediate Sex," *Selected Writings,* vol. 1, *Sex* (London: Gay Men's Press, 1984), p. 181.

2. Alan Cowell, "Vatican Attacks Population Stand Supported by U.S., Abortion and Homosexuality Are Seen as Major Issues at Talks in September," *New York Times,* August 9, 1994.

3. Alan Cowell, "Vatican Fights U.N. Draft on Women's Rights," *New York Times,* June 15, 1994, p. A–1.

4. Ibid.

5. Alan Cowell, "Legendary Big Italian Family Becoming a Thing of the Past," *New York Times,* August 28, 1993.

6. Rackham Holt, "Margaret Higgins Sanger," *Collier's Encyclopedia,* vol. 20 (London and New York: P. F. Collier, Inc., 1978), p. 403.

7. Norman F. McFarland, *The Miami Herald,* August 2, 1993. Excerpted from the July 1993 issue of the Orange County, California, diocesan newspaper, *The Bulletin.*

8. Lester Brown, "Natural Limits," *New York Times,* July 24, 1994, Op. Ed.

9. Associated Press, "World Population Must Drop to 2 Billion for Prosperity in Year 2100," February 22, 1994.

10. Lewis Bergman, "Perspectives on Provincetown," *New York Times,* July 17, 1983, section 10, p. 14.

11. Sam Roberts, *Who We Are: A Portrait of America* (New York: Times Books, 1993).

12. Anthony Lewis, "At Home Abroad: 'What Will Happen?' " *New York Times,* February 19, 1993.

8

How Fundamentalists Treat AIDS

Wouldn't it be great if you could only get AIDS from giving money to television preachers?

Elayne Boosler[1]

IN THE LAST chapter we saw how the fundamentalists' restriction on birth control has helped to fuel the AIDS crisis. This chapter explores how fundamentalist prudery and homophobia stifled aggressive efforts to combat this disease in the early days of the crisis, and continues to do so now.

Since the passage of years often muddies public recollections, let it not be forgotten that during the 1980s the Reverend Jerry Falwell, a darling of the Reagan-Bush administrations, went repeatedly on record as saying that AIDS was God's judgment against homosexual behavior. He was joined by a chorus of televangelists, including Pat Robertson, who repeated this contention. Both the Vatican and the Reagan White House, though less shrill, backed up the preachers with complimentary statements and behavior.

By 1987, it had become clearer to the public that AIDS was

not only affecting gay men, but that those infected worldwide were, in fact, primarily heterosexual. Banking on this new awareness, activists organized a demonstration against Falwell as he spoke to the Tiger Bay Club, a southern Republican organization, and begged a reporter covering the demonstration to go inside and to ask Falwell whether he was still teaching that AIDS was God's judgment against homosexuals. The reporter did so. The Reverend Falwell (knowing how short are the memories of his followers, and, squarely in the right wing tradition, never being shy about backtracking on matters that can later be easily tagged as nonsense) replied: "I think AIDS is God's judgment on America, not just on the homosexual society. Its rate is increasing faster now among heterosexuals than it is among homosexuals."[2]

To anyone familiar with the suffering caused by AIDS, such "judgments" by a fundamentalist god make of that god a vengeful beast so hideous that any mass murderer's tortures pale by comparison. To preach the existence of such a god is, in fact, as dangerous to society as the worship of a devil. Why? Because believing listeners are made, fundamentalists think, in that god's image, and either consciously or unconsciously they incorporate Jehovah's avenging spite and become thereby His instruments of retaliation. Early treatment of people with AIDS, including the hysteria that surrounded the burning in Arcadia, Florida, of a heterosexual household with HIV-infected children, as well as community judgments that fell on young Ryan White, were, as those families discovered, often encouraged by televangelist hate mongering.[3] How, one wonders, can a man stoop to such despicable depths as does the Reverend Jerry Falwell, when he calls AIDS "God's judgment on America"; how can he face frightened infected children whose young lives are blighted by the "religious" deceptions he manufactures, smugly trading on general ignorance simply to push forward his programs of institutionalized bigotry?

Because of the political influence Jerry Falwell wielded after proclaiming himself a new force with which to be reckoned, a virtual president maker, America's response to AIDS was criminally slowed. Ron Reagan, Jr., made bitter complaints against his father's mishandling of lives. The younger Reagan, explaining the necessity for wearing condoms, took part in an AIDS-awareness TV special and placed one over a banana, causing an uproar from the banana industry. In TV debates the younger Reagan challenged a right-wing Republican ideologue to admit that he believed that because a person is homosexual he could not also be moral. The ideologue appeared to be cornered. Ron, Jr., smiled confidently, a winning smile that nevertheless seemed to show his dismay that such a point even had to be argued. He explained that AIDS must not be thought fate's moral condemnation—that AIDS is nothing more or less than *a medical emergency.*

When asked why his father, the president, had not moved faster to curb the spread of AIDS, the younger Reagan replied that he himself didn't want to be blamed because he'd been after his father about AIDS for five years.

Speaking for a new generation, Ron, Jr., valiantly stood up to his terribly misled parents. To their annoyance he said what he believed to be true, courageously facing off against the kind of know-nothing, bigoted, hard-hearted, near-sighted fools, including his father, who must now, as AIDS death tolls rise, be made accountable for deliberate, ideologically inspired genocide and other heinous crimes against humanity.[4]

For such perceptivity, Ron Reagan, Jr., deserves the thanks of all who strive for self-direction as well as of all who have lost loved ones to AIDS. Many others deserve thanks, too, hundreds of thousands of others, living and dead. If the AIDS crisis has demonstrated anything, it is the strength and social cohesion of people of all sexual preferences in the face of extreme calamity. But the hollowness of Ronald Reagan, the actor-president, in his response to AIDS, the World War III of our time, must not be forgotten. With religious fundamentalism and several right-wing congressional members whispering social policy in his ear, he stupidly allowed the Specter of Death full reign over the republic; because he projected a swaggering macho persona that wasn't about to divert "Star Wars" monies to fighting a "gay" disease, he effectively led an entire nation into killing fields that far exceeded any battlefield in their horrors.

"Some Reagan administration supporters have gone on record as saying that AIDS is God's judgment on homosexuals," said H. Carl McCall, Chairman of the New York State Division of Human Rights; "but you have never heard one of them say that Legionnaire's Disease was God's judgment on the right-wing views of the American Legion."

The much-slowed social response to this hellish tragedy can be laid directly at the feet of the Radical Religious Right and its equally culpable gofers in the U.S. government.[5] Because the fundamentalist agenda has always sought control over all aspects of human sexuality, it continues to thwart the availability of *comprehensive* protections against sexually transmitted diseases. Fundamentalists have made politicians and others accomplices in their sick scheme to punish sexual behavior (through the denial of safer-sex protections) with death. They have spearheaded a series of diversions in response to AIDS, including mandatory testing with calls for quarantine, while allowing only one acceptable protective method: abstinence. They have flexed angry political muscle wherever there was talk of standard birth-control devices like condoms. No one in government would have dared suggest that along with the spending of billions on new bombers, society's taxes paid for defense might also be spent to encourage the commercial invention and promotion of a 100 percent effective condom.

While AIDS activists struggled against punitive fundamentalist schemes during the early years of the plague, hopes that AIDS might be contained by massive safer-sex educational programs were put on the back burner. Such programs, including talk of condoms, were recommended by Miami's avant garde group Cure AIDS Now, and could have put individual responsibility at their center, not state lock-ups and quarantines called for by a former governor (Robert Martinez, R-Fla.) and by leading fundamentalist theorists. Individual responsibility would have *turned citizen focus away from witch-hunts* for people with AIDS that were sought by the religious right and placed the duty of remaining virus-free with each individual. The question would not have been "Does this person have AIDS?" but rather "What am I doing to protect myself from AIDS?"

Following the 1977 rise of gay-baiter Anita Bryant, which led to the rabid institutionalizing of anti-homosexualism in fundamentalist circles, AIDS provided those circles with a new goad which was used promptly against America's gay communities. The connection between gay men and AIDS hysteria was thereby much heightened, thus turning national focus away from the menace to everyone posed by the virus, and trapping rational discussions in anti-gay rhetoric. A secret memo penned by the Reagan administration's assistant attorney general in charge of civil rights urged key Reagan officials "to polarize the debate on AIDS" so that AIDS would not be seen as a civil rights or privacy issue.[6] Edwin Meese, the attorney general, his aim steadied by fundamentalist pressures, fired the first volley at AIDS sufferers by saying, in 1986, that he would be satisfied if employers fired anyone suspected to be an AIDS risk.[7] This statement coincided with a conservative Supreme Court decision (*Hardwick* v. *Georgia*) against a gay male which seemed to allow Georgia police peeping rights into citizens' bedrooms. Next, William Bennett, former secretary of education and practicing Roman Catholic "values czar," stepped into the arena and insisted that sexual abstinence was the *only* way to prevent AIDS. The Reagan administration then sanctioned battles against condoms. Fanned by fundamentalist enthusiasms, mainstream newspaper articles assured heterosexual America it had nothing to fear from AIDS. Reverend Jerry Falwell led political struggles to reduce government AIDS spending, thus downplaying the need for emergency medical research into a cure, and for federal funds to help beleaguered states and suffering citizens. Representative Henry Waxman (D.-Cal.) said that the eighties would be remembered as "the AIDS decade" and that Reagan would go down in history as the president who did nothing about it.[8]

Indeed, the nation's secular AIDS experts began wondering why the president seemed eager to lose the AIDS war. The National Academy of Sciences focused on the administration's poor leadership on AIDS, characterizing it as "absent."[9] Then, the president's own AIDS commission chief, retired Admiral James D. Watkins, was belatedly appointed to investigate the virus and to suggest action. He wrote a report that flew in the face of right-wing religious lunacy, penning a chapter critical of Reagan's do-nothingism. The *New York Times* called this chapter "an unusual feature" for its lament about the "slow" and "sluggish" response by government to an emergency health crisis. Watkins said that such extreme tardiness would find us all without shelter should other severe national health threats arise. Thus did he castigate the president who had appointed him to his post.[10]

But Reagan retaliated. Though Admiral Watkins' Commission presentation became a photo opportunity for the campaigning George Bush, the admiral was not allowed to address media within the confines of the White House. All dressed up with no place to go, he delivered his AIDS speech in the White House driveway. "I'm embarrassed," said Watkins, "that we look like the Third World."[11]

While fundamentalists proclaimed sexual abstinence as God's advice on protection against AIDS, many made note of their "Falwellian" ploy as a simple-minded rush to judgment. They realized that fanaticism had begun to infect decision makers in some surprising quarters. There were bourgeois liberals who loved abstractions better than sex. There were bourgeois reporters who enjoyed telling us our dating patterns have already changed. And there were Republicans dreaming of a world where they would be safe from sex and its great challenges. All of them began to applaud what they called "The New Chastity." The party platform actually made *abstinence* a part of its written program.[12] Some may have reveled in the chaste estate, but they lived in a world apart.

Former Surgeon General C. Everett Koop wrote in his autobiography that the Reagan administration had forbidden him to mention AIDS until the plague had ravaged the land for five years. After AIDS became impossible to ignore, Dr. Koop was, among all Reagan's appointees, uncommonly and sanely outspoken about the disease. In the meantime, hysteria about it mounted, misinformation was rampant, and fundamentalists had a field day blaming homosexuals for self-destructing according to God's plan. If Representative Henry Waxman, who charged that Reagan's AIDS inaction was "almost willful," had known of the muzzle being put on Koop, he would have been able to say that it was *entirely* willful. But other heads of state, including the pope, were willful, too.

In 1989 Bob Kunst, director of *Cure AIDS Now* (the Miami organization lauded by Peter Jennings' TV serial reports, "AIDS Quarterly," as the most effective community-based AIDS organization in a state third-hardest hit by the disease), was invited to the first International Vatican Conference on AIDS. The previous year in Miami, Pope John Paul II evaded a reporter's question "Is AIDS God's judgment against homosexuals?" by replying that it is not easy to know God's intentions. The pope could, in a compassionate and civilized fashion, have laid the entire matter to rest by saying, "No, such an idea runs contrary to the kind of God I worship." But such was not the case. The same day the Vatican newspaper called AIDS "nature's sanction" against immorality, CNN showed Bob Kunst suggesting that the pope "shape up or ship out" of Miami.

Perhaps because his AIDS organization was on a list, or because Vatican organizers never saw the CNN report, Kunst received his invite to the Vatican AIDS conference. Once inside the holy site, he offered immediate commentaries to the press. "The Catholic Church," Kunst charged, "is so heavily into the condoms versus abstinence debate, they're really behind what's happening. My questions to church leaders are very simple. Where's the cure? Where's the cure? Where's the money for these things to happen? You are ignoring these questions."

Kunst carried his message, "Cure AIDS Now," and pressed it in the form of a button into the pope's hand. It was expected that the thousand scientists, church officials, theologians, and health workers invited to the conference would greet one another with the usual serene pleasantries. Thanks to Kunst and about forty-nine others, *Time* called the conference "a tense meeting" and a "ruckus," reporting that the hoped-for calm was "disrupted by dissident caucuses and angry charges and countercharges."[13]

Bob Kunst was at the center of the fray. The media quoted him addressing Archbishop Angelini, "This is the worst conference I've ever attended. It has been three days of gay-bashing." Kunst had shot a flaming arrow into a Citadel of Darkness while the whole world watched.

In the autumn of 1991 a savvy African chief of state upstaged President George Bush by stating that while he hoped to see an end to promiscuity, he also realized that practicality in the battle against AIDS meant that "condoms have a role." Vice-president Dan Quayle, however, criticized sports hero Magic Johnson for recommending condoms, insisting that abstinence is the only moral option for the unmarried.[14] New York City school board critic Mary Cummins, a heroine in the Reverend Kennedy "gay agenda" video, agreed with Quayle and pressed her campaign against condoms in sex education classes, ignoring the fact that AIDS had become a leading cause of death among those aged fifteen to twenty-four. She exacerbated the plight of young people like Alison Gertz, twenty-six, who died because of a single sexual experience she had had at age sixteen. Ms. Cummins did not want AIDS speakers addressing classes because, as she put it, "most such speakers are from the gay and lesbian communities."[15] Her statement not only made her an accomplice to the deaths of countless teens, but it reflected her spooky removal from the reality of heterosexual AIDS transmission.

We who are members of gay and lesbian communities have long warned that AIDS would soon devastate the straight communities as well, and, because of our experiences, we know best how to make clear the horror of AIDS and how to struggle for its elimination. The New York Health Department's projection of 100,000 AIDS deaths in the state by 1997 meant nothing to those like Mary Cummins, who insisted health professionals sign loyalty oaths pledging, if they addressed classes, to stress abstinence as the only answer to AIDS. Her name and that of John Cardinal O'Connor, who gave her moral support, should be noted when anguished parents collapse in despair as teen body counts rise.

As noted in chapter 7, the Roman Catholic Church works at cross-purposes with itself. While its chiefs disallow life-protecting condoms, Catholic volunteers help those in the terminal stages of AIDS to prepare for death. In many cases, people dying from AIDS give their last monies to a church that provides them with hospices and shelters built from necessity because of the very anti-gay prejudices that the church encourages. Lying on cots in these shelters, the dying faithful are served their last suppers by strangers because many virtuous Catholic families scornfully reject their sons and daughters.

In the spring of 1989, thirty-five Baptist ministers presented an award to Judge Susan Skinner, who had banished an AIDS patient from her courtroom, ignoring experts' findings that AIDS cannot be transmitted casually. "We thought that was admirable," said Reverend Richard Riley, pastor of Emmanuel Baptist Church in Ft. Myers, Florida.[16]

Local school boards, falling increasingly under fundamentalist influences, have proudly announced, as did one in Brevard County, Florida, that "condom use is not planned to be discussed by teachers in the classrooms," even though videos may give "some information" about these unmentionables. What if a student who is sexually active asks for details about condoms? Must the teacher be sworn, because of fundamentalist insanity, to silence? If condoms have a 10 percent failure rate, must the teacher bow before the Religious Right's mistake and say that *no protection is better than 90 percent protection?* Are not such school boards unwittingly participants in a scheme of fundamentalist retribution for sex by death?

Throughout the 1980s backwoods and big city fundamentalist preachers alike routinely put their own congregations at risk by preaching God's vengeance through AIDS. They are primarily responsible for the killer notion that AIDS is a gay issue and does not affect others. How, I wonder, must these congregations feel after discovering that their preachers have betrayed them; that this awful disease is no respecter of persons? What do preachers reply when members of their flocks disappear one by one? Can we continue to ignore AIDS as a leading cause of death among our young people? Must we continue, when practical sex education is censored, to watch helplessly as the young suffer and die? Is this sanity?

Future historians may look back on the fundamentalist prudery and closed-mindedness of our time as coinciding, unfortunately, with the most horrific of plagues. They will marvel at the billions spent on military weapons which failed to defend against the most insidious internal enemy ever.

This enemy is more than the AIDS crisis itself. It is the mindset that allowed the disease to rage unchecked for so long. Religious orthodoxy pursues a conformist, mind-dead policy of control that disallows individual autonomy, particularly in the area of sexual choice. The next chapter describes some ways in which gay men and lesbians can pursue a more humanistic program of self-determination in order to become truly autonomous individuals. Chapter 10 offers a picture of personal liberation for the future based on the vision of Walt Whitman, the great Poet of Democracy. Such liberation includes freedom from destructive male stereotyping, which is to be covered in chapter 12.

NOTES

1. Elayne Boosler, quoted in *Unnatural Quotations*, ed. Leigh W. Rutledge (Boston: Alyson Publications, 1988).

2. David Scruggs, *The Orlando Sentinel,* March 26, 1987, p. A–1.

3. Obituaries, "Ricky Ray, 15, Dies: Barred from school because of AIDS," *Washington Post,* December 14, 1992, p. D–8

4. S. Hallen, "If Papa Won't Preach It, Young Ron Reagan Will, with a TV Pitch Promoting Safe Sex," *People,* July 13, 1987, p. 38–40

5. "Enter the AIDS Pandemic: The Experts predict that 100 million will be stricken by 1990," *Time,* December 1, 1986, p. 45.

6. "Memo Urges Justice Department to Polarize Debate on Key Issues," *New York Times,* February 24, 1988.

7. Robert Pear, "Rights Laws Offer Only Limited Help on AIDS, U.S. Rules," *New York Times,* June 23, 1986, section A–1.

8. Associated Press, "Waxman: Reagan Failing on AIDS," August 10, 1986.

9. Philip M. Boffey "Expert Panel Sees Poor Leadership in U.S. AIDS Battle," *New York Times,* June 2, 1988, p. 1; also, Boffey, "Health Officials Fault U.S. on Response to AIDS Epidemic," *New York Times,* August 13, 1988.

10. Philip M. Boffey, "AIDS Panel Chief Urges Ban on Bias against Infected," *New York Times,* June 3, 1988, p. 1

11. Philip M. Boffey, "FDA Budge for AIDS Called Too Low," *New York Times,* February 20, 1988, p. A–9.

12. GOP 1988 party platform quoted in Leigh W. Rutledge, *The Gay Decades* (New York: Plume Books, 1992), p. 300. "Abstinence from drug use and sexual activity outside of marriage, is the safest way to avoid infection with the AIDS virus," said the platform.

13. "AIDS Ruckus in the Vatican," *Time,* November 27, 1989, p. 58

14. Karen DeWitt," Basketball on Capitol Hill, the Battle for AIDS Funds Heats Up," *New York Times,* November 9, 1991, section 1, p. 33.

15. Mary Cummins, quoted in "In Curriculum Fight, an Unlikely Catalyst," *New York Times,* November 27, 1992, p. B–1.

16. Carol Gentry, St. Petersburg *Times,* April 11, 1989, p. 1–A.

9

The Doctrine of the Autonomous Self

I take it for granted that you have a mind free from the superstition
which your teachers have sought to force upon you; that you do not
fear the devil, and that you do not go to hear parsons and ministers
rant. . . . I assume on the contrary that you have a warm heart and
for this reason I talk to you.

Peter Kropotkin (1842–1921)[1]

THE RAMSEY COLLOQUIUM, as mentioned in chapter 4, is a conservative ecumenical "think" tank composed of Catholic, Protestant, and Jewish theologians from many of America's foremost educational institutions, including Yale, Princeton, Amherst, Oberlin, Rutgers, Hebrew Union College, and the Catholic University of America. *First Things* (March, 1994) published the colloquium's attack on the gay and lesbian movement.[2] *The Miami Herald,* whose homophobic editorial department had supported the U.S. Supreme Court's 1986 decision *Hardwick* v. *Georgia* (see chapter 8) allowing police trespassing rights into bedrooms of suspected gays and lesbians, gave space to the attack. "The *Herald,*" said south Florida's gay newspaper, *TWN* (*The Weekly News*), "can and should print what it wants, but it must also absorb our criticism."[3]

The colloquium, which describes itself as "committed Christians and Jews," reveals, in its anti-gay, anti-lesbian, and anti-feminist rhetoric, a shameful lack of logic as well as the specific nature of its own worst fears. The signers of this document argue that the gay movement is more than a plea for civil rights. Their argument has arisen because same-sex love is a troublesome fly in the antiquated ointment of right-wing religious culture which, through the centuries, has tortured and murdered its opponents, divided humanity with heartless ignorance, and pushed twisted ideas of what it is that separates the sheep from the goats.

Using the phrase "pre-articulate anxiety" to describe America's reaction to homosexuality, colloquium members fail to see how part of that anxiety has been their own vicious creation. In attempting to label this anxiety "intuitive," they ignore major scientific and anthropological works, including *Patterns of Sexual Behavior* by Clellan S. Ford and Frank A. Beach; *Homosexual Behavior Among Males: A Cross-Cultural and Cross-Species Investigation* by Wainwright Churchill; *Homosexuality: A Cross Cultural Approach* edited by Donald Webster Cory; *The Construction of Homosexuality* by David F. Greenberg; and, of course, *Sexual Behavior in the Human Male (and Female)* by Alfred C. Kinsey, Wardell P. Pomeroy, and Clyde E. Martin. Many Americans do not share the intuitive anxiety touted by the colloquium. If citizens are uncomfortable in the presence of homosexuality, it is only because "religious" discourses, like those of the Ramsey Colloquium, inflame such fears and hatreds.

With blatant disregard for fair play, the Ramsey Colloquium's members call same-sex love "homo-genital contact," as if to say, as noted in chapter 1, that it is sex alone which motivates gay men and lesbians. Rightly, they link the fortunes of gay liberation to feminism, attempting thereby to connect it also with abortion, easy divorce, and adultery. They would return us to the "good ol' days" of coat hangers and annulments only for the super rich. Easy divorce conflicts with the colloquium's theology which would seem to prefer that unsuited married couples spend unhappy lives in quiet desperation.

In their anti-gay critiques, they write that we seek "liberation from constraint," which, I deduce, means we seek freedom from their dogmatic harnesses. True. But they also state, unforgivably, that gay people view the human body as little more than an instrument for the fulfillment of desire. This generalization is an outrageous lie. Since Socrates and Sappho, same-sex lovers have celebrated, in art and literature, our answer to this charge that our inclinations tend toward the flesh alone. The colloquium defines the family as "husband, wife and children joined by public recognition and legal bond" and as "the most effective institution for creating flourishing human communities," failing to take into account the sorry state of that institution today as well as the ever-climbing divorce rate.

"Finally," say these theologians, what gays want "rests on the doctrine of the autonomous self, which we believe to be a false doctrine." Since the colloquium gives no plausible explanation why autonomy is a "false doctrine," they leave it to us who are gay to address the accusation. It would seem that it is this fact of autonomy, which I do not deny, that annoys them most. They do not want individuals able to throw off their oppression and who make personal attempts to arrive at personal truths. Instead, they want a flock of followers who behave like sheep, not sturdy, independent mountain goats who wander on their own less-traveled paths. They oppose individual autonomy. On this ground alone they are vile enemies of freedom.

Gay men and lesbians can best respond to this charge by hoisting even higher the banner of self-command, the doctrine of the autonomous self, in order to help ensure that none, whether heterosexually or homosexually inclined, remain weak followers of false cults, but become instead the proud creators of individualistic lives, sharing with others, wherever possible, the fruits of those joyous energies which self-reliance brings.

The concept of self-reliance, though not peculiar to America, is central to the American dream. Ralph Waldo Emerson's essay "Self-Reliance" pointed the way: "Whoso would be a man," wrote Emerson, "must be a non-conformist. . . . No law can be sacred to me but that of my nature. . . . I am ashamed to think how easily we capitulate to badges and names, to large societies and dead institutions."[4] Emerson's famous essay points, as did the Buddha five hundred years before Christ, to the central concern of each person. Buddha, reportedly, had said:

> *It is not what others do or do not do*
> *that is my concern;*
> *It is what I do and what I do not do,*
> *that is my concern.*[5]

Emerson elaborated on the Buddha's teaching:

> What I must do is all that concerns me, not what the people think. This rule, equally arduous in actual and in intellectual life, may serve for the whole distinction between greatness and meanness. It is the harder because you will always find those who think they know what is your duty better than you know it. It is easy in the world to live after the world's opinion; it is easy in solitude to live after our own; but the great man is he who in the midst of the crowd keeps with perfect sweetness the independence of solitude.[6]

"Self-Reliance" examines ephemeral concepts to which a misled citizenry looks for its succor. It clearly states that "a greater self-reliance must work a revolution in all the offices and relations of men; in their religion, in their education, in their pursuits; their modes of living, their association, in their property, in their speculative views."

Emerson appreciated the fact that "reliance on Property, including the reliance on governments that protect it, is the want of self-reliance." Similarly, reliance on instructions given from any religious hierarchy is just as much a want of self-reliance. Only those religious traditions that encourage a dependence on self, including the Society of Friends (Quakers), Buddhism, Unitarian-Universalism, and Vedanta, can, without embarrassment, contain in their worldviews such statements as Emerson's. But those religious traditions teaching members to be *followers* would seize from individuals the very core of their individuality, making of them unquestioning slaves to systems that demand allegiance to exterior powers. In theological terms the difference between an *immanent* (internal or intrinsic) god and an *external* god becomes crucial. The latter sort of deity encourages dependence. Only what Quakers call "the inner light" leads to an immanent godhead, and thence to self-governance.

The concept of an external god always wreaks havoc on society. Not only does this concept focus an individual's meditations away from self-scrutiny, but it rests the whole of moral conduct on a dubious external approval. When external divinities fail to appear or to convince, as is the dilemma of the church today, a populace that does not focus instead on the worth of its inner guide floats adrift. Since fundamentalist and orthodox dogmas, including that of the atonement, work to dissolve the need for searching self-examinations, each individual's moral compass spins awry. The exterior gods maintain an eery silence while

those who have been trained to look upward and outward
develop, because of wrong bearings, no inner strengths. Society's children are not taught to ask questions but to accept
answers. Thus deprived, they look upward for help, failing to
appreciate that true help must be self-administered.

NB

"Very well, then," objects the timid theologian; "but individualism leads to anarchy. If humanity fails to pay homage to
our outmoded holy scripture, if there is no divinely established guide, there will be moral chaos." This argument shows
how little confidence its proponent feels for longterm pros-
pects in a dogma-free community, where an individual's independent awareness takes precedence over obeisance to nonsense. It ignores the reality that many cultures have thrived
socially without having heard a whisper about God's peculiar
plan, his demand that there be a blood sacrifice of Himself.

"If Christianity were only stupid and unscientific," said
Robert G. Ingersoll,

> if its God was ignorant and kind, if it promised eternal joy to
> believers and if the believers practiced the forgiveness they
> teach, I, for one, should let the faith alone. . . . But there is
> another side to Christianity. It is not only stupid, but mali-
> cious. It is not only unscientific, but it is heartless. Its god is
> not only ignorant, but infinitely cruel. It not only promises
> the faithful an eternal reward, but declares that nearly all the
> children of men, imprisoned in the dungeons of God, will
> suffer eternal pain. This is the savagery of Christianity.[7]

Jesus himself, among others, provided a sound moral base
for social interaction: "A new commandment I give unto you,
that you love one another." This suggestion does not need any
supernatural sanction. It is a recurring theme in most religious cultures. Zealous claims to moral high ground, however,

have been badly damaged by the fact that the Judaeo-Christian tradition has provoked rather than calmed storms of misdirected human passion. The adherents of this tradition, with only a few *individual* exceptions, have been, in the judgment of many historians, the cause of untold miseries. Proving that intolerant religious crusades bring an end to whole societies makes much more sense than blaming homosexuality for any such collapse. One need not return to former centuries to confirm this fact. Present-day governments, including that of the United States, tremble before the onslaughts of fundamentalist meddlers and terrorists.

Orthodox focus, because it draws the attentions of believers away from self-care, putting them into the "hands" of an exterior god, and because it has long treated the human body as a center of corruption, has effectively erased the principal starting place where autonomy begins. If, as Maria Montessori tells us, young children make every attempt to be self-regulating (see chapter 6), "religious" influences soon squelch such self-regulation. Religious objections to nudity superimpose garments that hide the body, allowing the faithful to ignore its very existence. Believing the body to be a mere seat of temptation, religious zealots, unable to discuss its natural functions without embarrassment, often disregard the basics needed for its proper maintenance.

The religious right's long-standing objection to public school sex education stems directly from its refusal to relinquish its stranglehold on this personal dimension, fearing that secular views may lead to *individual decision making* outside the boundaries of established dogma. The condom, dividing sex from reproduction, becomes the foremost symbol of such decision making. The orthodox argument, namely, that mere knowledge about condoms promotes immoral behavior, falters before the national calamities facing us: a million pregnancies annually among unmarried teens, as well as the rising teen death count due to AIDS. If the religious right had even a shred of decency, its adherents would, instead of blocking free-choice clinics, be distributing condoms in church.

"By dint of *not* following their own nature," writes John Stuart Mill of those who merely conform, "they have no nature to follow: their human capacities are withered and starved: they become incapable of any strong wishes or native pleasures, and are generally without either opinion or feelings of home growth, or properly their own." Wherever there are no autonomous selves there reside the living dead. If they have made no effort to self-create (other than through reproduction), they have lived not their *own* lives but lives programmed for them by others. Religious fanaticism seemed on the wane during the last three centuries but now "religious" enthusiasms return to feed like vultures on the intellectually impoverished. The fanatics have regrouped and any degree of power granted them will, one can be sure, be used against genuine human sociability. When the World Congress of Religions issued invitations to the centennial meeting of that august body, Southern Baptists and other fundamentalists declined, refusing to place their precious "truths" on display in a meeting hall where they would be unable to make claim to an undeserved superior status.

So accustomed are the religiously acculturated to obedience that many would actually wait for permission from others before embarking on personal quests for truth, unable to grasp that only *one's own permission* is needed. Social interaction can be improved if one's insights into oneself first point the way. It is not belief in some proposition requiring blind faith that enhances one's ability to communicate but, rather, personal insight. Such insight appreciates that others are traversing their own paths. Each self-aware individual works to develop an empathetic awareness that will open him to under-

standing those in his community. Worthy philosophic in-
quiries, of which fundamentalists seem incapable, must begin
with tacit admissions of ignorance, a willingness to say that
one comes armed only with a few good guesses. But understanding quickly evaporates when one believes oneself the
possessor of absolute truth. The "religious" zealot has come to
this place to set you right. Yours must be the contribution of a
head that nods in agreement, or, as history shows, that head
becomes, much to the surprise of its owner, dispensable.

The first step toward autonomous selfhood lies in becoming aware of the cultural confusions that envelop and misdi-
rect each citizen. Freedom of the self from demoralization
derives from a unique kind of self-observation that is not judgmental. A meditative state is often recommended so that self-
understanding can arrive, and it does if one strives to integrate a clear awareness of the best in one's inner life with
one's daily behavior. This requires an avoidance of either
pompous or defeatist self-deceptions. Any attempt to start a
child on its way to self-discovery must work from the premise
that the primary obstacle to self-awareness is the flippant but
common assumption that one already has self-knowledge.

In a world where the autonomous self is sovereign, there is
liberty to do anything that does not stand in the way of others'
well-being. There must be freedom to express one's own perspective, right or wrong. Even the fundamentalists, who know
nothing of such liberty, are due such free expression; but
since they know the truth already, they will allow no provoca-
tive controversies. This is too bad. Independent thought and
its exchange with others is the only relevant path to any truth.
Without it there is only blind assertion. Religious fanatics,
armed like parrots with repetitive assertions, are unable to
give actual accounts of their doubts. Where else, except in
mental prisons, curled like scorpions in bedroom slippers, are

the "religious" souls who would silence all independent thought, making sure that every person bows before the absurdities and contradictions of "divinely revealed" authorities? These censoring souls stand ready to condemn those who fail to pay heed to their nonsense. Politicians and businessmen think they are required to camouflage any honest contempt for religiously inspired inanities. Seldom do they express doubts over dogma. Thus we are witness to clouded bamboozlements drifting everywhere across our horizons.

The autonomous individual would reject such an arrangement, preferring instead to express the fact that he does not accept as his own the common man's myths. Such an individual cannot be a hypocrite and pretend to believe what he or she does not believe. This, too, would be abject cowardice. The self-actualizing person prefers a world where ideas and concepts enjoy that variety of free expression the religious right is forever trying to vanquish. That person who best perceives self-worth must carefully and regularly look for the good, the true, and the beautiful in his own skeptical way.

Few have spoken of the joys of the autonomous self more clearly than Robert G. Ingersoll:

> When I became convinced that the Universe is natural, that all the ghosts and gods are myths, there entered into my brain, into my soul, into every drop of my blood, the sense, the feeling, the joy of freedom. The walls of my prison crumbled and fell, the dungeon was flooded with light, and all the bolts, and bars, and manacles became dust. I was no longer a servant, or a slave. There was for me no master in all the wide world, not even in infinite space. I was free. Free to think, to express my thoughts; free to live to my own ideal; free to live for myself and those I loved; free to use all my faculties, all my senses; free to spread imagination's wings; free to investigate, to guess and dream and hope; free

to judge and determine for myself; free to reject all ignorant and cruel creeds, all the "inspired" books that savages have produced, and all the barbarous legends of the past; free from popes and priests; free from all the "called" and "set apart," free from sanctified mistakes and holy lies; free from the fear of eternal pain; free from the winged monsters of the night; free from devils, ghosts, and gods. For the first time I was free. There were no prohibited places in all the realms of thought—no air, no space, where fancy could not spread her painted wings—no chains for my limbs; no lashes for my back; no fires for my flesh; no master's frown or threat; no following another's steps; no need to bow, to cringe or crawl, or utter lying words. I was free. I stood erect and fearlessly, joyously, faced all worlds.[8]

Autonomous thinking destroys fundamentalist theory. Religious fanatics do not want *thinkers*, they want *believers*. When their beliefs become hard to swallow, apologists must try to explain. Promoters of the Book of Mormon know no shame as they insist that golden tablets (found with an angel's help and later returned to an undisclosed location in Elmira, New York) were reputedly translated from an ancient tongue with the use of miraculous spectacles given by the angel to the Latter Day "prophet" Joseph Smith.

The sorry state of fundamentalist apologetics becomes clear as it promotes clumsy attempts to disprove evidence of evolution. Fundamentalist academics, mostly from small sectarian colleges, narrate films meant to disprove any estimate of the earth's age that goes beyond a few thousand years. It must not be forgotten that only within the current decade has Pope Paul II posthumously returned the excommunicated astronomer Galileo to church membership. It is little wonder then that the pope's organization is sometimes known as "the Flat Earth Society." Perhaps three hundred years hence some pope may think better of women as priests and of gay men and lesbians as deserving the same rights accorded others. But I, for one, have no wish to wait for the "holy" father's tardy insights.

To those who would cast aside the primitive concept of "divine revelations" and who favor the development of an insightful autonomy, I would recommend the affirmative philosophies of Democracy's muse, Walt Whitman. Nowhere else in world literature, I would argue, is there a more comprehensive examination or celebration of selfhood than in *Leaves of Grass,* and especially in Whitman's longest poem, "Song of Myself," as I describe in the next chapter.

NOTES

1. Peter Kropotkin, "An Appeal to the Young," in *The Essential Kropotkin: A General Selection from the Writings of the Great Russian Anarchist Thinker,* eds. Emile Capouvya and Keitha Tompkins (New York: Liveright, 1975), p. 10.

2. The Ramsey Colloquium, "The Homosexual Movement," *First Things: A Monthly Journal of Religion and Public Life,* No. 41, March 1994.

3. Jack Nichols, "God's Gift to Atheism," *TWN* (*The Weekly News*), Miami, March 23, 1994.

4. Ralph Waldo Emerson, *The Complete Essays and Other Writings of Ralph Waldo Emerson* (New York: Modern Library College Editions, 1953), p. 145.

5. *The Dhammapada,* trans. P. Lal (New York: Farrar, Straus & Giroux, Inc., 1967).

6. Emerson, *The Complete Essays,* p. 150.

7. *Ingersoll the Magnificent,* ed. Joseph Lewis (Austin, Tex.: American Atheist Press, 1983), p. 110.

8. Robert G. Ingersoll, *Faith over Agnosticism: The Field-Ingersoll Discussions* (Austin, Tex.: American Atheist Press, 1983), pp. 74–75.

10

Walt Whitman's Vision

I am personal. . . . In my poems, all revolves around, concentrates in, radiates from myself. I have but one central figure, the general human personality typified in myself. But my book compels, absolutely necessitates, every reader to transpose himself or herself into the central position, and become the living fountain, actor, experiencer himself or herself, of every page, every aspiration, every line.
                                                            Walt Whitman[1]

NEEDLESS FEARS ARE whipped up by religious fanatics as they impose their vision of what constitutes "rightful" community, insisting it be based on certain narrow dogmas. This community, they say, is incompatible with individual autonomy. Such fears were addressed more than a century ago in the opening lines of Walt Whitman's extraordinary *Leaves of Grass*:

> *One's self I sing, a simple separate person,*
> *Yet utter the word* Democratic, *the word* En-Masse.[2]

155

What follows these lines is an entire book celebrating the love of self, which in turn leads to the ability to care for and embrace others, effectively melting this illusory division. Whitman's nigh-revelatory mind-state, while it eschews dogma, sounds passionate affirmations of self-supremacy, a "simple separate person" rising effortlessly and integrating with the many. This mind-state gives a powerful impetus to social harmony. *Leaves of Grass,* to my way of thinking, has long provided the most profound answer to fundamentalist lies about gay movement aims. In the second edition of *Leaves,* Whitman made clear his intention, namely, to produce a spellbinding but nondogmatic scripture. Calling attention to the fact that we live in a world of many revealed religions, he signaled that he, too, would "descend into the arena." Like the prophets of old, Whitman reclaimed mighty truths, confidently depending on nothing more than his power with words to disseminate a revolutionary worldview.

As early as 1973 gay activists carried Whitman's *Leaves of Grass* to the twenty-sixth annual Conference on World Affairs hosted in the shadows of the Rocky Mountains by the University of Colorado. Some had long been sounding Whitman's name, regularly publishing assessments of his importance. At the conference the significance of Whitman's vision was emphasized again, indicating that his major work should be understood as a primary source for the gay liberation movement. Whitman, let it be noted, was already in the libraries of the nation's public schools. It is only a matter of time before fundamentalists will discover that the Poet of Democracy proselytizes without embarrassment for same-sex love, using hypnotic cadences passionately trumpeting the utter deliciousness of sexual contact, and welding together, as does no other thinker, many categories, including soul, sex, gender, and nature, the rational and the mystic, the material and the spiritual, the one and the many. While no single gay man or lesbian, no matter what their breadth of experience, can speak for all other homosexually inclined people, university students attending the conference were told that Whitman is a great precursor and fountainhead of prophecies, visions, and attitudes, both toward society and the self, that are at the very basis of the gay, lesbian, and bisexual liberation movements.

Barely a quarter century has passed since the Colorado Conference, and yet mainstream gay America has yet to rise to the challenges posed by Democracy's poet. Many have yet to discover the fact of Whitman's profound influence on pioneering gay liberation thinkers in other lands and on brilliant heterosexually inclined artists, dancers, and authors, including Robert Henri, Isadora Duncan, and Waldo Frank. Not without significance was the testimony of a great-grandfather of gay liberation, Edward Carpenter (also a champion of nineteenth-century feminism), who described himself as a moon reflecting Whitman's sunlight. Some have doted on a section of *Leaves of Grass* titled "Calamus," Whitman's vision of the social implications of same-sex love. Others have pondered the sixth line in the *Leaves* which says, "The Female equally with the Male I sing."

America may be ripe for a Whitman revival, as shown when, in 1992, New York City's cultural institutions, with appropriate fanfare, led a multitude of festivities honoring the one hundredth anniversary of the poet's death. Many notables crossed the homo-hetero barrier in their effusive praise, just as the poet would have wished. They were catching up to Whitman's foreign admirers by calling him America's greatest poet, a station he'd long ago prophesied would be granted him. He'd bravely ignored the well-intentioned advice of Ralph Waldo Emerson, who had pleaded with Whitman to remove from his poetry such bold and expressive celebrations of sexuality. As perceptive a man as he was, Emerson lacked Whitman's physical dimension because he approached the material world as an emanation of spirit. Whitman's emphasis began at the opposite pole, stressing that it is through the material world, particularly our bodies, that we experience what may be called spiritual awareness. He saw how any contrary view had led to an unhealthy ignoring of the body. "I keep as delicate around the bowels," he wrote in words that shocked the puritanical, "as I do around the head and heart." Such complete self-awareness is, sadly, still uncommon. It is just such a spirited reclamation of the physical self that stands in contradistinction to old-fashioned fundamentalist metaphysics.

NB

The implications of Whitman's reclamation of the physical body are central to the general well-being of both individuals and society. It initiates a fundamental revolution in consciousness, opening the door to a self-awareness that has remained unknown to those suffering an anti-material worldview which labels the body a nonentity or a center of corruption. Whitman called himself the poet of the body and the soul. "Divine am I inside and out," he proclaimed, "the scent of these armpits aroma finer than prayer. This head more than churches, bibles, and all the creeds. . . . There is that lot of me and all so luscious."[3]

It was Whitman's celebration of what his body had allowed him to perceive that differentiated him from other poets, still mired in dry intellectual complexities, lacking the excitement of that physical joy which gave Whitman an intense sense of his own nature.

Americans, unlike other cultures, often find it difficult to approach poetry. Its song, incantation, magic, and passion have seemed to be missing for them, partly, perhaps, because many twentieth-century poets, particularly T. S. Eliot, have too much celebrated despair. Owing to cultural blindness, and a fear that poetry is sissified, Americans rob themselves of the spirited sources that buoy other cultures. Many therefore experience a poverty of spirit, ignoring the enrichments provided by their far-sighted cultural giants.

As same-sex liberation was taking its first optimistic steps during the late sixties and early seventies, its champions had no way of knowing how much despair and pessimism would infect a not-so-distant future. The spell of 1960s countercultural triumphs still filled the air in those heady days like early morning dew. As an antidote to future pessimism, however, and to its resultant cynicism, it seems to me that the Whitman tradition remains well suited to our rapidly changing American civilization. It throbs with a sense of magic. It is a great primal chant, stepping over labels such as male and female, national and international, human and nature, and fusing them in a harmony of unrhymed rhythm, free and jubilant. It reaches out and embraces existence with an unequaled positive joy.

This is not to insist that Whitman's is strictly a homosexual tradition. But his *Leaves of Grass* includes homosexual inclinations without fear and with great love. Whitman, however, was much larger than his homosexuality alone, and he simply used it, as he used everything, to touch others and to make them self-appreciative. His sexuality was blended with his whole feeling for life's larger dimensions. He understood that what he felt within was good, that his own body was a miracle. And in a very important sense, Whitman was a prophet of male liberation. When he wrote, "I celebrate myself and sing myself, and what I assume you shall assume," he meant that the ecstatic feelings he entertained could become—with awareness—the natural property of every man and woman. The poet's celebration of *adhesiveness*, his term for the cementing of the social body through same-sex comradeship, is central, as Whitman himself knew, to his gospel of democracy.

Edward Carpenter, the renowned English man of letters who made a journey across the Atlantic specifically to meet the American poet, writes:

> Walt Whitman, the inaugurator, it may almost be said, of a new world of democratic ideals and literature, and—as one of the best of our modern critics has remarked—the most Greek in spirit and in performance of modern writers, insists continually on this social function of "intense and loving comradeship, the personal and passionate attachment of man to man." "I will make," he says, the most splendid race the sun ever shone upon, I will make divine magnetic lands. . . . I will make inseparable cities with their arms about each other's necks, by the love of comrades." And again in *Democratic Vistas*, "It is to the development, identification, and general prevalence of that fervid comradeship (the adhesive love at least rivaling the amative love hitherto possessing imaginative literature, if not going beyond it), that I look for the counterbalance and offset of materialistic and vulgar American Democracy, and for the spiritualization thereof. . . . I say Democracy infers such loving comradeship, as its most inevitable twin or counterpart, without which it will be incomplete, in vain, and incapable of perpetuating itself."[4]

The heterosexually inclined American writer Waldo Frank, best known, strangely, to Latin Americans for his incisive reflections on Spanish culture, considered himself a philosophic child of Walt Whitman's. In the United States the significance of Frank's challenging thought remains almost unknown, in spite of such prophetic works as *The Re-Discovery of America,* and his championing of the pioneering photographer Alfred Stieglitz, whose lover was painter Georgia O'Keeffe. In a letter to the annual Whitman celebration in 1923, Frank wrote:

There is no such thing as the spirit without the body, as the thought without the form. If the thought and spirit of Walt Whitman are at all to prevail and function in our American life, they must take shape, they must become part of the body of American experience. . . . Whitman alone was vast enough, athletic enough in intellect and vision, to measure the parabolic growth of America into its present promise of universality. . . . I look on Whitman today not so much as a cultural possession of America . . . we have not yet won him . . . but rather as a Challenge. He is a challenge to our literature, to our criticism, to our institutions, to our entire social polity, to grow up to his own universal Norm. The prophets were such a challenge to the Hebrews . . . and they accepted it. Let us do likewise.

Therefore I say that a mere passive love of Whitman is not enough. We must work very hard and very deep upon the message of Whitman and upon its application to ourselves, if he is indeed to become our cultural possession. . . . It is by such work that the Poet will become organically part of ourselves, and that the essence of his creation will become nourishment for the future race of Poets that Whitman previsioned in our land.[5]

When Frank wrote these words Whitman had been dead only thirty-one years. During the poet's lifetime other notables celebrated him unabashedly, including not only Emerson and Thoreau, but Robert G. Ingersoll, the silver-tongued infidel whose oratorical criticisms of orthodox religion turned nineteenth century clergy on their heads. Ingersoll's little-known tribute to Whitman, "Liberty in Literature," was delivered in the poet's presence, and the orator collected that night the then hefty sum of eight hundred dollars, which he gave away gratefully to assist Whitman through the vicissitudes of old age. A happy heterosexual family man, Ingersoll also addressed those gathered at Whitman's funeral and prophesied that the poet would be remembered many centuries hence. "Today we give back to Mother Nature, to her clasp and kiss, one of the bravest, sweetest souls that ever lived in human clay. . . . And I today thank him not only for you but for myself for all the brave words he has uttered. . . . Millions will walk down into 'the dark valley of the shadow' holding Walt Whitman by the hand. . . . I loved him living, and I love him still."[6] Oscar Wilde, the famed Victorian playwright, also visited the poet and advised scholars to study him, if not for his poetry, then for his philosophy, for, he wrote, "he is the precursor of a fresh new kind of man."[7]

Whitman's intense spiritual draw has since been noted by scholars in every land. His sense of worldwide solidarity was celebrated in a large Moscow hall in 1955 on the hundredth anniversary of the first edition of *Leaves of Grass*. In 1971 the University of Nebraska published a notable book by V. K. Chari, an Indian professor who made clear the likenesses between Whitman's self-awareness and that found in India's Vedantic tradition.[8] Witter Bynner, translator of the Chinese sage Lao Tzu, compared attitudes found in the Chinese thinker's work to those contained in the *Leaves*.

For many years only a few American scholars attempted to approach this homoerotic genius, unnerved, probably, by their own and their culture's homophobic stance. In recent times, however, major works of literary criticism have appeared quickly in succession, and with each new statement the good gay poet's reputation is enhanced. A 1991 study, *Disseminating Whitman: Revision and Corporeality in* Leaves of Grass, by Michael Moon lights new paths for Whitman scholarship, showing how the poet promulgated a radical conception of corporeality, bypassing the limitations of nineteenth-century prudery, a condition akin to fundamentalist prudishness today.[9]

Walt Whitman's prose diagnosed the maladies of his era. In 1873 he described the corruptions in America which stood in the way of a truer democratic flowering. What Whitman said then remains current:

> I say we had best look our times and lands searchingly in the face, like a physician diagnosing some deep disease. Never was there, perhaps, more hollowness at heart than at present, and here in the United States. Genuine belief seems to have left us. The underlying principles of the States are not honestly believ'd in, (for all this hectic glow, and these melodramatic screamings,) nor is humanity itself believ'd in. What penetrating eye does not everywhere see through the mask? The spectacle is appalling. We live in an atmosphere of hypocrisy throughout. The men believe not in the women, nor the women in the men. A scornful superciliousness rules in literature. The aim of all the *literateurs* is to find something to make fun of. A lot of churches, sects, &c, the most dismal phantasms I know, usurp the name of religion. Conversation is a mass of badinage. From deceit in the spirit, the mother of all false deeds, the offspring is already incalculable. An acute and candid person, in the revenue department in Washington, who is led by the course of his employment to regularly visit the cities, north and south and west, to investigate frauds, has talk'd much with me about his discoveries. The depravity of the business classes of our country is not less than has been supposed, but infinitely greater. The official services of America, national, state and municipal, in all their branches and departments, except the judiciary, are saturated in corruption, bribery, falsehood and maladministration; and the judiciary is tainted. The great cities reek with respectable as much as nonrespectable robbery and scoundrelism. In fashionable life, flippancy, tepid amours, weak infidelism, small aims, or no aims at all, only to kill time. In business (this all-devouring modern

word, business,) the one sole object is, by any means, pecu-
niary gain. The magician's serpent in the fable ate up all the
other serpents; and money-making is our magician's serpent, remaining today sole master of the field. The best class
we show, is but a mob of fashionably dress'd speculators and
vulgarians. True, indeed, behind this fantastic farce, enacted
on the visible stage of society, solid things and stupendous
labors are to be discover'd, existing crudely and going on in
the background, to advance and tell themselves in time. Yet
the truths are none the less terrible. I say that our New
World democracy, however great a success at uplifting the
masses out of their sloughs, in materialistic development,
products, and in a certain highly deceptive superficial popular intellectuality, is, so far, an almost complete failure in its
social aspects, and in really grand religious, moral, literary
and esthetic results. In vain do we march with unprecedented strides to empire so colossal, outvying the antique,
beyond Alexander's, beyond the proudest sway of Rome. In
vain have we annex'd Texas, California, Alaska, and reach
north for Canada and south for Cuba. It is as if we were
somehow being endow'd with a vast and more and more
thoroughly appointed body, and then left with little or no
soul.[10]

No physician or preacher could more accurately have put
his finger on our social troubles, and Whitman's solutions,
woven through his works, stand light years beyond fundamentalist ravings. His patriotism, obviously, is tempered by an
unsparing eye and by strong common sense. He brings to bear
his full appreciation of issues surrounding the emancipation
of women, the equalization of homoeroticism, and the prob-
lems posed by the rise of technological and narrowly rational-
istic structures.

Great national poets appear only irregularly on history's

horizons. Robert Burns still speaks to the heart of Scotland, his values, in spite of a strict Presbyterian climate, permeating and profoundly affecting the populace there. Mystic poets like Hafez, Saadi, and Rumi do the same for Iran, in spite of the present seizure of the government there by repressive fundamentalists.

Walt Whitman's perceptions are, I believe, indispensable to his countrymen and to his admirers in other lands if humanity is ever to march optimistically into the future. The Whitman tradition places its admirers in harmony with what is called Eastern Wisdom, including Zen, Vedanta, and the Tao, encouraging the necessary mating of East and West, of absorbent Mother Asia and of our own penetrating sphere. Whitman remains of central importance because he has already captured many cultured hearts who self-identify as egalitarian heterosexuals, and yet he speaks in like measures of the equal place that must be fashioned for same-sex lovers. He chants:

> *I will sing the song of companionship,*
> *I will show what alone must finally compact these,*
> *I believe these are to found their own ideal of manly love,*
> *   indicating it in me,*
> *I will therefore let flame from me the burning fires that were*
> *   threatening to consume me,*
> *I will lift what has too long kept down those smoldering fires,*
> *I will give them complete abandonment,*
> *I will write the evangel-poem of comrades and of love,*
> *For who but I should understand love with all its sorrow and*
> *   joy?*
> *And who but I should be the poet of comrades?*[11]

Recent Whitman studies unveil what keen thinkers such as Waldo Frank, Edward Carpenter, and others knew instinctively, that the poet had provided humankind with a cultural grounding astounding for its reach and breadth. Whitman's political worldview beckons to his countrymen to walk self-contained as individuals at his side or ahead of him. Meanwhile, fundamentalists, who oppose this degree of self-direction, can only tremble.

NOTES

1. Walt Whitman, Introduction, *Leaves of Grass: "The Deathbed" Edition* (New York: The Modern Library, Random House, 1921), p. vii.

2. Walt Whitman, "One's Self I Sing," *Leaves of Grass* (Amherst, N.Y.: Prometheus Books, 1995), p. 9.

3. Ibid., "Song of Myself," p. 49.

4. Edward Carpenter, *Selected Writings,* vol. 1, *Sex* (London: Gay Men's Press, 1984).

5. Waldo Frank, *Salvos* (New York: Boni and Liveright, Inc., 1924), p. 276.

6. Robert G. Ingersoll, *Liberty in Literature: Testimonial to Walt Whitman* (New York: The Truth Seeker Company, 1890).

7. Oscar Wilde, quoted in *The Artist as Critic,* ed. Richard Ellman (New York: Random House, 1968), p. 125.

8. V. K. Chari, *Whitman in the Light of Vedantic Mysticism* (Lincoln: University of Nebraska Press, 1964).

9. Michael Moon, *Disseminating Whitman: Revision and Corporeality in* Leaves of Grass (Cambridge, Mass.: Harvard University Press, 1991).

10. Walt Whitman, "Democratic Vistas," *WHITMAN Poetry and Prose,* texts selected by Justin Kaplan (New York: Literary Classics of the United States, 1982).

11. Whitman, "Starting From Paumanok," *Leaves of Grass* (1995), p. 21.

Winning against Fanaticism

Experience witnesseth that ecclesiastical establishments, instead of maintaining the purity and efficacy of Religion, have had a contrary operation. During almost fifteen centuries has the legal establishment of Christianity been on trial. What have been its fruits? More or less in all places, pride and indolence in the Clergy, ignorance and servility in the laity, in both, superstition, bigotry, and persecution.

President James Madison, 1784[1]

THE CENTURIES-LONG BATTLE to keep religious fanaticism at bay has created heroic traditions in every land as well as numerous methods to fit each reoccurring struggle. In the United States this struggle has produced significant manifestoes from every field, starting with Thomas Paine's *Age of Reason,* a work still remarkable for its trenchant dynamism. Among Americans who have followed directly in Paine's footsteps are Robert G. Ingersoll, Mark Twain, Clarence Darrow, H. L. Mencken, Gore Vidal, and a host of others who have turned their wit, observation, reason, and experience against rotting dogmas.

In Great Britain this tradition includes reformer Charles Bradlaugh; the famed biologist, former UNESCO Director Julian Huxley; and such world-class philosophers as David Hume and Lord Bertrand Russell. In the first rank of France's anti-clericals stood the great writer Voltaire, who worked over-time to keep Catholics and Protestants from killing one another, as well as Ernest Renan, whose sympathetic biography of Jesus approached the first Christian in a naturalistic framework, while downgrading St. Paul and his theories. In the East, Iran produced the skeptic-poet Omar Khayyam. And half a millennium before Jesus the great Taoist mystic Lao Tzu struck a direct blow to fundamentalism in *The Way of Life* (*Tao Teh Ching*), whose opening lines say:

> *Existence is beyond the power of words*
> *to define:*
> *Terms may be used*
> *But none of them absolute.*[2]

India has given us Salman Rushdie, who, in his *Satanic Verses*, casts doubt on the holy book of Islam, earning him a *fatwa*, or death sentence for heresy. As of this writing Mr. Rushdie remains in hiding. More recently, the heroine-writer Taslima Nasrin came before a Bangladeshi court on the charge of defaming Islam. Her fanatical detractors formed a hundred-man death squad to kill her. Nasrin's "crime" was to suggest an alternative to Islam's four-wife system, namely, that women be allowed to have four husbands. The Islamic hierarchies, patriarchal to the core, treat Ms. Nasrin's suggestion as the worst sort of abomination. The Far East, including China and Japan, has long nurtured those anti-dogmatic strains of Zen which refuse all conceptual formulations, dismissing them as mind-made.

The twentieth century has seen religious zeal in the United States wax and wane in its effects on the citizenry. The reign of fundamentalist influences, especially in the South, gave early rise to a variety of concerns, including an ongoing struggle against the teaching of evolution which reached its first peak in 1925. Failure of fundamentalists in the 1930s to enforce their demands to outlaw the teaching of evolution gave a black eye to their causes which, until the late 1970s, seemed a permanent mark. They found themselves regrouping only after noticing the initial political success of a self-proclaimed "born again" Democratic presidential candidate, Jimmy Carter. Their cause, however, was championed by Republicans who rallied behind them to ban abortion and who heartily welcomed the addition of their newly oiled political machinery which began to reach into former Democratic enclaves, turning fundamentalists throughout the Bible Belt into active Republican enthusiasts. At its presidential conventions the GOP demonstrates its continuing commitment to fundamentalist issues, loudly promising a continuing antagonism to pro-choice advocates as well as virulent hostility to any suggestion of civil rights for gay men and lesbians. Former vice-president Dan Quayle led one Republican charge by posing as the champion of fundamentalist interpretations about what it means to belong to a "legitimate" family. Single-parent families and homosexual couplings stood, from this perspective, markedly outside the pale.

The early nineties have dealt major blows to the fundamentalist campaign against pro-choice clinics, including negative publicity about the bombings of these facilities. The Supreme Court has had to step in to prevent clinics from being blocked by fundamentalist crusaders, and, as of this writing, there have been shameless murders of two physicians and a clinic guard and the brutal killings of two clinic workers.

Since, however, cash flow lining preachers' pockets from anti-abortion hysteria is presently on the wane, many have turned to gay-bashing as a more effective guarantor of funds. One result is the successful encouragement of such bashing by bigots in the general populace. Openly gay men and lesbians have been murdered in alarming numbers, our homes burned and vandalized, our jobs threatened, and our right to assemble or associate put in ever-increasing jeopardy. Because fundamentalists continue to treat AIDS as a gay/morality issue, political sluggishness impedes proper sex education as well as modes of disease prevention, adding what many see as numerous charges of second-degree murder to already existing first-degree fundamentalist crimes.

If, as the Reverend Jerry Falwell boasts, he offers something "ten million worlds better" than Iran's current theocratic regime, it behooves us to reflect on how young Iranian men and women are presently eluding Iranian fundamentalist police. Lacking opportunities for opposite-sex contact now taken for granted in the West, their plight is not unlike that which long affected America's homosexual communities. If young men are caught with young women without written proof that they are related by blood, both are subject to severe punishments. For weekend fun, Iran's young people have been reduced to climbing through remote mountainous areas where they meet in secret and enjoy romantic trysts over innocent picnics minus headscarves, veils, and *chadors* (leg-length robes). Still the morality police pursue them doggedly, complaining as they do of the arduous task God has assigned them. One is reminded of similar fiascoes in the United States. Here, on a remote beach, naturists, or nudists, gather for similar picnics with their families, while seething fundamentalists complain bitterly of moral decay and prevail upon a similarly minded county sheriff to badger these harmless revelers; but though they have managed to fill entire courtrooms with naturists, judges have repeatedly found the nudists innocent. The American Civil Liberties Union (ACLU) was summoned to their defense.

Iranian fundamentalists insist on the death penalty for those convicted of having homosexual relations. Gay men are given four choices: hanging, stoning, being dropped from the highest point, or being halved by a sword. Christian fundamentalists in the United States, who include Southern politicians, also advocate the death penalty for homosexuals. The Christian Reconstructionist Movement has been cited by Neighbors Network, a nonprofit organization that monitors hate groups, as a leading force in Dixie promoting anti-gay violence. According to Neighbors Network,

> The great strength of these groups is their intimidation and terrorism that they practice, and that they can only practice if they remain anonymous. If you expose them and their leadership to public light it immediately begins to erode their ability to intimidate and frighten people. . . . We are simply pointing out that these people are hiding behind religion. They are using religion as a cloak for this political agenda they want to push. And they ought, at least, to be honest about what their goals are.[3]

A fearful dilemma facing American society is that hate groups masquerading under fundamentalist religiosity are rapidly infiltrating local governments. By hiding the nature of their campaigns, as well as their belief systems, they are, nevertheless, able to take over school boards, city and county commissions, and other public institutions, counting, as other political candidates do not do, on the zealous hands of secretive church officials and their members, all of whom are con-

scripted to do necessary political groundwork, including enve-
lope stuffing, petitioning, and canvassing. They are able, without scruples, to bypass constitutional restrictions that keep a
much-needed divide between church and state By doing this
they maintain their tax-exempt status as long as they make an
empty show of respecting this divide. "The stories of million-
dollar salaries, million-dollar jets and houses from Malibu to
Miami," said Rep. Byron Dorgan (D.-N.C.) at a congressional
hearing on televangelists, "not only raise eyebrows but raise
some questions of reporting and accountability."[4]

The degrees to which fundamentalist churches become
tools for fund raising that has nothing to do with religion
ought to provide notable measuring devices by which their
right to retain tax-free status is judged. A political columnist's
work, for example, is taxable. Church literature, though it
clandestinely promotes fascist views, is not. Political videos like
those hawked for twenty-five or more dollars by the Reverend
D. James Kennedy (see chapter 5), which are sold in great
quantities, are purchased at a set price as a so-called donation
to the ministry, even though by any reasonable standard the
amount of a donation should be determined not by the ministry but by the individual making the donation. Otherwise, a
fair observer would contend, it is a sale. These videos are filled
with anti-gay or anti-free-choice propaganda, not to mention
fundamentalist diatribes against Supreme Court decisions, the
ACLU, and other matters quite outside what one might call
legitimate religious concerns.

Among the anti-gay front groups to which fundamentalists
give unstinting support is the American Family Association
(AFA) founded by Donald Wildmon of Mississippi. Its
branches reach every state where homosexuality is still regarded as a crime, and its purpose has been to cancel civil
rights for gay men and lesbians in those municipalities which

have granted us equal protection under the law. By labeling such protection "special rights," the AFA hoped to mislead citizens into believing that the gay and lesbian movement seeks more than equality. Using misinformation, and innuendoes and distortion, the AFA and other affiliated groups stir up unbridled misunderstandings and ill-will toward a vast homosexual citizenry.

In Florida the AFA has been headed by a self-confessed former pornography addict, David Caton, whose addiction cost him, according to his own account, three hundred dollars per month in magazines and videos.[5] After deciding he'd been "born again," Mr. Caton and the AFA set about to reverse a newly enacted Tampa city ordinance protecting gay men and lesbians from abuse in both housing and employment. For a time Caton was successful until it was found that an undue number of his petitions were worthless, and thus the protective city ordinance was reinstated by the courts. Foiled, Caton then attempted to deny any further categories of discrimination whatever, and he hoped this could pass, without mentioning homosexuals, as a referendum on Florida's ballots. The state's Supreme Court, however, stopped Caton midway by explaining that the AFA initiative was flawed. He has since attempted to reverse gay anti-discrimination ordinances in other Florida cities where they have been passed. Is his spiteful activity an accurate portrayal of a truly Christian theme?

Similar activities spawned by the AFA are presently underway in a number of states. Referendums limiting civil rights for gay men and lesbians have been successful in various local municipalities, though the AFA has yet to inaugurate its discriminatory hopes on a state level. Benighted citizens in Colorado and later in Cincinnati, Ohio, voted to rescind equal rights for homosexuals, but the judiciary moved quickly to squash their attempt at legalized bias, returning those civil rights seized by bigots. President Clinton, expressing an alarm with which we who are fighting these state and city battles are well-acquainted, was moved to say, in a February 14, 1994, letter to the Gay and Lesbian Victory Fund, that those trying to legitimatize anti-gay discrimination are *gravely mistaken* about the values that make America strong. "The essential right to equality must not be denied by ballot initiative or otherwise," he wrote. The U.S. Supreme Court backed this gay and lesbian-protection viewpoint with a strongly worded decision (*Romer* v. *Evans*) delivered on May 20, 1996, concerning the Colorado amendment: "Amendment 2 classifies homosexuals not to further a proper legislative end but to make them unequal to everyone else," wrote Supreme Court Justice Anthony M. Kennedy for the Court's majority of six. "This Colorado cannot do. A state cannot so deem a class a stranger to its laws. Amendment 2 violates the Equal Protection Clause." Thus, the Court foiled long-range fundamentalist schemes by declaring unconstitutional the Colorado state constitutional provision that had nullified civil rights protections for homosexuals. "This is the most significant victory to date," said pioneering gay activist Franklin E. Kameny, who brought the first gay civil rights case before the Supreme Court in 1961, though it was not heard by the court. "But the decision could have been stronger."[6]

The single organization most successful in routing these fundamentalist ploys has been the ACLU. Its large loose-leaf briefing book, prepared by the ACLU Lesbian and Gay Rights Project, has been used to combat anti-gay ballot initiatives and is an arsenal of much-needed strategies for gay activists nationwide. The history of these now crumbling initiatives, an analysis of their courses, and recommendations about what to do make the ACLU briefings an invaluable source.

The courts provide one route for combating religious

fanaticism. Another is gay readiness to express, humorously if possible, forgiveness for those "Christians" who seek to defame us. A telling demonstration of such forgiveness was given by Bob Kunst, who had once succeeded in making Anita Bryant—the third runner-up beauty pageant contestant, orange juice ad lady, and gospel singer turned rabid gay-baiter—look foolish in a nationally televised TV debate in 1977. A decade later, when Ms. Bryant's fortunes had declined and she was singing for her supper at various trailer parks, *The Orlando Sentinel's* Sunday magazine, *Florida,* quoted both Kunst's remembrance of Bryant and her thoughts about him:

> Bob Kunst's voice rises with delight when he hears of Anita Bryant. Does he remember Anita Bryant? Does he ever! He's going to call his autobiography *From Anita to AIDS.*
>
> Bob Kunst is a flamboyant, headline-grabbing Miami Beach homosexual activist. Kunst's big cause is curing AIDS. His big cause ten years ago was the Dade County gay rights ordinance. And Anita Bryant-baiting.
>
> Anita Bryant is singing at mobile home parks? Great! Maybe Bob Kunst will get a few friends to picket the shows.
>
> Anita Bryant—says Bob Kunst—was the best thing to happen to gay rights. She single-handedly galvanized gays. He can still pull a derisive laugh from a crowd by just saying her name.
>
> "We loved her," he says, "She has such potential. She's got such a powerful voice—but she sings the wrong tunes. I always said, she was my best friend.
>
> "Tell her this: I'd love to manage her career. I'll make her a new folk hero. We could fill the Orange Bowl, Shea Stadium. I'll give the money to AIDS, she can give it to her church. I'll come with her to her mobile homes and pass out condoms. I'll make her a star. Tell her."
>
> Anita Bryant receives this message as she bounces back

to the Punta Gorda Holiday Inn. It's past midnight, she's crossed the day's mobile home parks from the itinerary.

"Bob Kunst!"

Anita Bryant jerks up straight. The name hits her like an electric shock.

"Bob Kunst! What did you talk to him for? That nincompoop!"

Her expression is horrified. Her eyes open wide. Her lipsticked mouth slackens. She barks a few short laughs.

"'The Orange Bowl! Ha! I don't find him funny. At all. He represents a very painful part of my life."[7]

Unfortunately, the excitable Ms. Bryant herself represented a very painful period in the lives of those about whose same-sex affections she so viciously lied. Her unhappiness at hearing Kunst's name was, from a gay activist's standpoint, a compliment. From Kunst's standpoint, there was no reason to hold on to his anger or to express bitterness or blame. The orange juice matron had gone the way of the dodo. Seeming to visualize herself as a Christian martyr, Ms. Bryant reportedly expressed fears that homosexuals might assassinate her. To this Gore Vidal replied: "The only people who might shoot Anita Bryant are music lovers."

A frontal assault on fundamentalist beliefs can be accomplished *sub rosa* without references to gay activism. What is needed is the outright willingness from all sides of the affectionate and sexual continuum to launch missiles filled with comic exposés of fundamentalism. Theatrical wit makes the most potent weapon. Many heterosexuals, bright freethinkers including humanists, Unitarian-Universalists, Ethical Culturists, agnostics, and atheists, would welcome such creative endeavors. The arrival of video as an easily distributed medium makes it safe for actors to play, as Dana Carvey, as Church

Lady, did, a leading role in satirizing narrowness of mind and the effects of harmful religious dogmas.

Filmmakers John Binninger and Jacqueline Turnure have produced a twenty-minute parody of Reverend Kennedy's gay agenda titled *The Straight Agenda.* "It begins with a Cronkite-like narrator intoning overpopulation statistics over scenes of starving people and really bad weather—the cost of 'heterosexuality out of control.' Talking heads add authority to the message: Audrey (comedienne Suzy Burger) was trapped in the hetero cycle of 'dating, marriage, children and divorce' (a classic clip shows her pregnant and shopping for liquor.)"[8]

A comedy trio calling itself Funny Gay Males is featured on videos and in books. Jaffe Cohen, Danny McWilliams, and Bob Smith treat conventional religions with gay style, telling how they discovered early that "religious" trappings could be traps. In *Growing Up Gay: From Left Out to Coming Out,* they recount their amusing personal experiences within Judaism, Protestantism, and Catholicism.[9]

To aid in the development of such satire, the best contemporary collection of humorous *directional* suggestions may be found in the late comedian Allan Sherman's *The Rape of the Ape.* This book is among the funniest and most original extravaganzas ever written about social prudery. Sherman is remembered best, perhaps, for a simple camp song, "Camp Granada": "Hello Muddah, Hello Faddah, Here I am at Camp Granada. . . ." But it is *The Rape of the Ape,* a masterful romp through time, which puts him in the front rank. *APE* is an acronym for American Puritan Ethic, and Sherman dissects this "ethic" and its dogmatic or fundamentalist base with 448 pages of the finest, most trenchant wit.[10]

The nineteenth-century speeches of Robert G. Ingersoll await resurrection and redelivery by accomplished actors. Twelve volumes of that great orator's critiques of organized religion comprise the funniest, most compelling and damaging tirades against religious fanaticism ever composed. In debates, he was pitted against Roman Catholic Cardinal Edward Manning; William E. Blackstone, the Prime Minister of Great Britain; and a distinguished American divine, Henry M. Field, D.D. Ingersoll's devastating and razor-sharp slicing of the Old Testament is called *Some Mistakes of Moses,*[11] a book and also a shorter lecture. In his autobiography Clarence Darrow tells us that he was among those young lawyers who went regularly to hear Ingersoll, principally to mimic his style, though, as Darrow reports, "Nobody ever spoke as Ingersoll did." Ingersoll's good cheer and kindness were infectious, and when he died Mark Twain said of him that he'd grieved only at the death of his own daughter more than he did at Ingersoll's passing. The orator's material is alternately poetic (Shakespeare was his Bible and Robert Burns his hymn book) and colloquial, injecting sly humor akin to Twain's. "Do you believe the rib story?" Ingersoll intoned, pretending he was the angel at heaven's gate. Then in the tone of a man who hopes to enter, he replies, "You mean the Adam and Eve business? Why bless your soul, of course I do. My only regret is that there are no harder stories in the Bible so I could show my wealth of faith." Ingersoll was well acquainted with most of the great geniuses of world literature, and his viewpoint, as an avowed agnostic, was both ethical and compelling in the extreme. He said:

> I belong to that great church that holds the world within its starlit aisles; that claims the great and good of every race and clime; that finds with joy the grain of gold in every creed, and floods with light and love the germs of good in every soul. . . . Neither in the interest of truth, nor for the benefit of man is it necessary to assert what we do not know. No

cause is great enough to demand a sacrifice of candor. . . . I combat those only who, knowing nothing of the future, prophesy an eternity of pain—those only who sow the seeds of fear in the hearts of men—those only who poison all the springs of life, and seat a skeleton at every feast.[12]

The struggle against religious fanaticism is ongoing. Many more thoughtful Christians, as well as conservative Republicans like Barry Goldwater, are openly appalled by the spectacle of so many fundamentalists expending their energies and monies to deprive others of their rights. Some gay activists are approaching the mainstream clergy and asking them to publicly disassociate themselves from the genocidal tirades of their fellow "Christian" spoilers. This is important work. Gay activists who are sympathetic to Christian concerns should arm themselves with knowledge, arrange private consultations with nonfundamentalist clergymen, and explain that it is their Christian cause which suffers when it becomes clear that some of their so-called brethren are engaged in shameless hate-mongering. Are Presbyterians, for example, satisfied that Reverend D. James Kennedy stirs intergroup animosities under the Presbyterian banner? It is high time that other men and women of the cloth, those with the integrity that Kennedy lacks, stand up bravely and be counted. Otherwise it may be necessary for members of the gay community less sympathetic to the standard-brand Christian belief system to create and distribute their own videos, including speeches effectively satirizing and critiquing that system. I myself, favoring the oratorical approaches of Robert G. Ingersoll, would welcome such a move. During the 1980s, while fundamentalists had full access to the White House, there was only one effective opposing national voice, that of a man in drag, namely, Dana Carvey as the Church Lady appearing regularly on "Saturday Night

Live." Who was the Church Lady? "Oh, I don't know," Carvey's character might have replied, "Satan?"

NOTES

1. James Madison, *The Great Thoughts,* ed. George Seldes (New York: Ballantine Books, 1985), p. 261.

2. Lao Tzu, *The Way of Life According to Lao Tzu,* trans.Witter Bynner (New York: Perigee Books, 1972).

3. Kathy Alexander and Gayle White, "Focus on American Vision: Christian Reconstructionists Advance a Radical Belief That Includes Support for Cobb's Anti-Gay Resolution," *Atlanta Constitution,* July 5, 1994, section B, p. 5.

4. Michael Isikoff, "Evangelists Defend Funding Tactics: Decry House Hearings as Dangerous Precedent," *Washington Post,* October 7, 1987, p. C–1.

5. Mike Thomas, "Are Gays Rights a Civil Right?" *Orlando Sentinel, Florida* magazine, Sunday, July 18, 1993, p. 8.

6. George Ferencz, "Gay Movement Earns Milestone Legal Victory," *Florida's Hot Spots!,* Memorial Day Issue, 1996, p. 58.

7. Barbara Stewart, "Being Born Again: Anita Bryant Resurrected, She's Starting Fresh," *Orlando Sentinel, Florida* magazine, Sunday, February 21, 1988.

8. Chris Baker, "Heterosexuality on the Rampage," *Baltimore Alternative,* February 1996.

9. Funny Gay Males, *Growing Up Gay: From Left Out to Coming Out* (New York: Hyperion, 1995).

10. Allen Sherman, *The Rape of the Ape* (Chicago: The Playboy Press, 1973).

11. Robert Ingersoll, *Some Mistakes of Moses* (Amherst, N.Y.: Prometheus Books, 1986).

12. Robert Ingersoll, *Faith or Agnosticism: The Field-Ingersoll Discussion* (Austin, Tex.: Atheist Press, 1988), pp. 74–75.

Straight Men and Gay Men

It's comin yet for a' that
That man to man the world o'er
Shall brithers be for a' that.

Robert Burns[1]

IN THE TWO decades since the first feminist critiques of male roles, many remain painfully conscious of how pressing are the odds working against not only *inter-gender understanding,* but, as a result, *human survival.* Logically, along with feminism's phenomenal growth, there should also have been a role revolution among men counterbalancing and complementing changes taking place in women's lives. Instead, after sparking only a few rounds on talk shows, a film or two like *Mr. Mom,* and sitcom jokes about machismo, especially on "Home Improvement," there's been, in spite of early warnings about the pressing need for redefining male roles, an eery silence about such liberation. Sporadically there is vague talk in women's glamour magazines about men becoming more "sensitive," or a nod here or there to a manly show of feelings or of men being able to help around the house or to weep without embarrassment. But these superficially treated issues have sidetracked gut discussions and have blurred a more comprehensive view. America's dominant folk art, the news media, has failed, for the most part, to understand either the substance or the gravity of male issues. The fledgling men's movement, divided into four disparate wings, has limped along, leading nowhere. One wing acts as a counterreaction to feminism and attempts to reclaim male privilege. Another is supportive of feminism, but weighted down by academics short on strategy and who too openly parrot feminist theories. They have thus failed to communicate a sense of true social urgency, making instead mere armchair challenges. A third, better-publicized men's faction follows poet-guru Robert Bly, who leads seeker-after-truth-male coteries into rural encampments where they discuss myths and attempt to make "needed" connections with primitive interior images of some sort. Such tactics, however, merely provide media with a novelty feature, making it unnecessary for the TV and radio networks to demonstrate any serious commitment to male-lib concerns.

The fourth, and by far the largest, group has been spawned, over the last two years, in right-wing waters. Known as the Promise Keepers, it capitalizes on male-bonding needs, attempting to route those needs into "Christian" channels. Massive gatherings in stadiums throughout the nation focus also on easing the distress males know as current economic woes lean heavily on their self-images. Their protector-provider roles need shoring up, it seems. The Promise Keepers have found success as they celebrate their own brand of male camaraderie, all under the spell of conventional religious glee. Male camaraderie is thereby defined and sublimated into "proper" channels to "protect" Christian men from the truly serious meanings behind the equality of the sexes. Such a group, as the other men's organizations, is probably a mixed bag of positive and retrogressive effects, allowing antiquated pundits to gently scoff at what has now become society's underlying need, *an effective challenging of male roles, and, as has occurred among feminist women, an increase in bonding.* Emphasizing men's movement miscarriages in the 1980s, Gross, Smith, and Wallston write:

> In the past decade it has failed to cohere and prosper as a nationally influential movement. In contrast with its frequent comparison, modern feminism, it has not succeeded in significantly altering the fabric of society, in suggesting new legislation, or even in providing an alternative avenue for the personal frustrations of millions of American men.[2]

There has been little or no attention given to the fact that a saner society will flower only when men liberate themselves from contrived, socially fabricated prohibitions, cultural straitjackets, and mental stereotypes that control and inhibit behavior through arbitrary definitions of what it means to be a man. When it becomes clear that certain macho attitudes are destructive, men will react differently toward each other, with different expectations, priorities, purposes, and awarenesses. In a world where men were bold enough to question their assigned roles as women do, any dominating master-director, requiring others to support his force-fed power plays, would be treated as anachronistic and counterproductive.

But many straight and gay males have been caught in the web of old-fashioned male posturing. Some have tried to extricate themselves from its withered strands, but the culture has given them little or no support. Men are *encouraged* to preserve such rigid postures (even with only vague notions of what they mean) with greater urgency than they are taught anything else. Thus, the patriarchy, harboring harmful illusions of male dominance, remains the greatest impediment to social reform. Receiving its support from the Judaeo-Christian tradition, basking in the approval of dog-eat-dog capitalism, lacking empathy for the underprivileged, having too little environmental empathy, the old patriarchal order runs roughshod over whole populations; its adherents hope for *survival of the fittest* profits, celebrating their tough-guy theatrics which, if left unchecked, will lead to planetary doom. How important is it to beat others at the game? To seize instead of to share? To compete instead of cooperate? To an inquiring avant garde that hasn't yet despaired, to those who see through to patriarchy's profound social implications, it follows that opening male role options is a major revolutionary activity. The old male prescription is, both in personal relations and in social effects, more limiting, more anxiety-provoking, and more insidious than any other kind. The values at its base encourage violence and destruction.

The modern woman, in her struggle toward equality, must still pass through powerful male checkpoints. Many ape male roles, following male-dominant values. Even many gay males, because they react against pre-Stonewall limp-wrist images, have, at times, become overly emphatic about demonstrating that they themselves have highly valued macho characteristics. They are likely to say, "I am a man. I'm not a drag queen. People think gays like me are effeminate, but I'm not. I'm just as masculine as the next guy." Straight neighbors, "the next guys," also suffer the scourge of keeping up butch appearances simply to pass muster.

Male role conditioning has led to a monumental brutalization of life which males are taught to inflict and to experience. Cultural demands for traditional manliness are hangovers from previous ages, and are presently near, if not at, the core of the conditioned male's agonies. His intimate behavior, a rigid love life or lack of it, is clearly a microcosm of many social ills. Human survival requires a shedding of his calcified self-image and the creation of new routes better suited to self-awareness and the resultant empathy needed for human inter-action. The conventional male's poker face, signaling his denial of the reality of feeling, destroys general hopes he may develop empathy, the primary key to encompassing awareness. This is because he often fails to make emotional connections with others. Such failure leads him directly into warfare, whether in the bedroom or on the battlefield. The time for major changes among males may wait until society has had its fill of "put up your dukes" violence. Then, perhaps, perceptive men will trespass the domains of their crumbling holy of holies, treading with bold feet on formerly sacrosanct areas, inspecting, questioning, and doubting retrogressive "mascu-line" concepts, and discovering that these are, in fact, a crip-pling disease.

The fundamentalists' support for the patriarchal system finds them unwittingly supportive of other aspects of socially acquired masculine roles, including those kowtowing to insti-tutionalized violence. A jealous god, orthodox man's exem-plar, is often a violent god, as the character of Jehovah amply demonstrates. A husband who expects obedience is less likely to spare the rod and spoil the wife. Pat Robertson and his Christian Coalition politico, Ralph Reed, worry plenty about reproductive and sexual violations, for example, but seem content not to critique the military-industrial complex. Fun-damentalists fearing too much media violence almost always show an equal or greater concern about explicit sex. When the subject is men's and women's roles, too few ask why, in the United States, 95 percent of all violent crimes are committed by men. When the question of the "weaker" sex arises, few ask why men, as a class, die eight years sooner than women. A front-page headline of the *New York Times* says "abuse has replaced romance" in the relations of present-day male teens toward peers of the other sex.[3] No one asks why *Rambo* may, because of box office successes, enjoy ten lives, or why *The Terminator* seems unwilling to self-destruct. And what do popular games (both on the field and in video arcades) reveal? That violent confrontation makes for "good" spectator sports, whether teammates battle or leave it to their fans to do the honors. The pre-fight boasting of championship wrestlers would provide clever macho comedy routines if only more viewers could better appreciate the satire. Violence is endemic. Threats of violence constitute "excitement." Violent fictional deaths remain constant enticements as entertainment. If there is no truth to the axiom "monkey see, monkey do," then why, it must be asked, is violent crime on a meteoric rise among youth?

Answers to these dilemmas, found through study of the lesbian and gay men's cultures, reveals an evolving, still-living tradition passed on to the present by visionary muses who were aiming at a healthier, more fluid, and affectionate society. For over a century this tradition has grown, nurtured in part underground by poets, activists, mystics, and avant garde artists. Going beyond single issues, this tradition focuses instead on the part the gender revolutions play within the larger realm of human unfolding. If the personal is political, then it may be that in a man's most intimate relations (a fundamentalist's way of demanding the subjugation of his wife, for example), he may give clues as to the breadth of his political acumen. Not only fundamentalists but many culturally assimilated gays as well will also balk at this long-standing gay-feminist tradition, because, as Republican New York Mayor

Rudolph Giuliani put it, "Gays and lesbians disagree with each other just like everyone else does." And, as I've already stated, *there is no specific gay agenda.*

Even so, there is this unique tradition that reaches within and outside "gay" issues, pointing not to a world of heterosexual or homosexual isolates, but to affinity and social contacts which flow beyond old dualisms and celebrate a human rather than a specifically gay or straight dimension. Whether exclusivists on either side of the fence admit it or not, heterosexuality and homosexuality are not exclusive states of being, but each is part of a natural human continuum, just as they have always been. A reasonable agenda, therefore, would advance the idea, from either end of this continuum, that there is no *them.* There is only *us!* If we who are gay men and lesbians continue to regard ourselves as part of a minority, we will suffer from a kind of inferiority complex that overrates the other end of our continuum. Must we continue to beg for our rights as we walk, hat in hand, toward what seems to gay dualists a powerful, institutionalized heterosexual monolith? Scanning the daily newspapers helps those with timid natures to face facts: the heterosexual monolith is in ruins, with male/female relations having arrived, in many locales, at frightful and lonely stalemates. There must exist an alternative to such loneliness. The tradition therefore announces that the "homosexual" end of the continuum must no longer be passive or obsequious. To be so would be tacitly to admit an inferior status. The time has come to offer not pleas for tolerance, but passionate invitations to those who would stifle the love that dared not speak its name. Whom should we address? Let's start with gay men in priestly clothing. Or, perhaps, fundamentalist preachers, those tortured closet cases who haven't had the coming-out courage shown by Mel White, former ghostwriter for Jerry Falwell and Pat Robertson. Of gay priests it can be stated casually that there are, as the pope knows, untold but massive numbers. Let these priests come out of their closets and declare, as straight priests do, that they want sanctification for their secret relationships with each other. Or do they fear losing their cushy appointments and job security?

To see same-sex lovemaking as the sole property of an isolated group is to assume a reactionary pose, signaling a clinging to the indefensible status quo. Homosexual feelings are not merely those of an isolated minority, forever beyond the experience of humanity's masses. The ability to love one's own gender is the necessary property of every person, one that has long been waiting to be discovered on levels other than the sexual, but *including the sexual*. To propel itself it need rely only on its exuberant expressions, attractive because they are open-minded, bold, flexible, loving, and joyfully unembarrassed.

For far too long has the gay and lesbian part of the human continuum self-identified as a persecuted few. Now it is time to point out to persecutors that by condemning same-sex relationships they are condemning part of their own potential. In a nuclear age men who express feelings only through competition, avoiding other males emotionally as if avoiding a plague, are, in reality, *causing* a plague whose symptoms include disconnection, alienation, and mass isolation, muddling the concept of brotherhood with unconscious homophobic anxiety and leading, therefore, to a more tense and dangerous world. Viewed in a planetary perspective, the homosexual taboo becomes a foremost barrier to much-needed brotherhood or comradeship.

At this juncture the connection between the gay and lesbian liberation movement and society at large becomes clearer. Out-of-the-closet persons remind sexually repressive cultures of their own psychologically stifling restraints, which erect barriers to communication and cause anguish, keeping millions from leading emotionally fulfilling lives. Gay, lesbian, and bisexual liberation should, in my opinion, open doors not only for those homosexually inclined but for millions of others who, on various levels, live lives stunted and maimed by same-sex fears. The straight person who discriminates because fears of close same-sex affinities are rampant, is as much in need of liberation as any gay person who may fear, dislike, or treat the other sex unfairly.

The death knell for the kind of masculinity that must always prove itself, striking out, posing, and boasting, is long past due. One's personal responses are unwitting political statements. The male who recoils from passivity, for example, shows he knows little about its strengths. Stances such as receptivity or passivity have many forms, such as listening. Men who take only the active role—talking, for example—fail to *hear* what's going on, being unconsciously deaf to what proceeds around them. Fear of being thought womanly (recognizably subservient) has led men to reject women's reputed stances or virtues. Of course there are no "masculine" or "feminine" virtues. There are only *human* virtues. The rejection of receptivity, unfortunately, creates whole populations of deaf, dominating men and mute, submissive women. Women who flaunt their active side in the bedroom often frighten those men taught to expect absolute cooperation from passive receptacles. The old role long ago enshrined the giving of directions as, principally, a male prerogative. One can be a drill sergeant on a military base or in bed.

The macho code has been carried beyond the blustering stereotypical male. Where physical domination is no longer a prerequisite to social survival, traditional machismo has emerged on new levels, proving male identities through intellectual posturing and combat, technological dominance and control, and narrowly defined realities that reduce experience to measurements and statistics. "In our culture money equals success," says Dr. Robert E. Gould. "Does it also equal masculinity? Yes—to the extent that a man is too often measured by his money, by what he is 'worth.' Not by his worth as a human being, but by what he is able to earn, how much he can command on the 'open market.' "[4]

Men in positions of control in commercial enterprises, including the media, academia, and government, have, while unaware of their own conditioning, guided and controlled access to thought on matters that surround what is called, with confused scorn in some circles, the "sexual revolution." The result has been frustrating. What men deserve—truly satisfying sexual/loving relationships and experiences—has been fogged in by piecemeal intellectualizations about sexuality. Men have, without meaning to do so, added to their own alienation through destructive emphasis on bedroom technique. Second-rate profiteering media hype has brought about sex lib talk leading to fantasies, "adult" bookstores, and skinflicks. A world of sexual/loving sanity, aware of the deliciousness of sexuality and of affection's healing powers, needs more than a focus on physical positioning. It needs a healthy psychological attitude.

In 1976 an early men's conference drew participants from many states. Gay and straight- identified men (straights comprising the overwhelming majority) experienced what for many was a spiritual reawakening. Tears came to many eyes. Men hugged, kissed, and danced merrily with each other after a weekend aimed at getting over homophobic fears. The anxieties of the straight-identified majority were successfully quelled. For the gay-identified minority, the new step seemed almost magical, bespeaking an evolutionary development. The majority saw how they'd been denied the joys of closer relationships with other men not only because of the gay taboo, but because their old roles had demanded that they compete, measuring off against one another, racing, getting ahead. Harboring such values, they had formerly been distrustful of each other, as well as guarded and inhibited. Personal communication had paled before impersonal raps about teams and scores with an emphasis on dry details that skirted direct expressions of feeling. There had been too much deliberateness in their relationships, destroying playfulness and spontaneity. Among these men, fearful of touching each other, relationships had withered because their programming had, for the most part, called them to be calculating, defensive, and unfeeling. Previously their friendships had become linked with having mere sidekicks.

This conference was an early attempt made by men who were, in a sense, learning to walk. Unforeseen developments have since shaped what we know of men's liberation gatherings today. There was a different kind of euphoria experienced by African-American males at the first Million Man March, one called by the leader of the Nation of Islam, a Moslem fundamentalist group. With its crafty entry into the male bonding field, Promise Keepers' orthodox Christian approach fills a hunger among men, even if, in my opinion, inadequately.

In a May 23, 1969, column a pioneering gay male journalist and activist, the late Lige Clarke, launched one of the earliest critiques of machismo. He was murdered in February 1975 in a hail of gunfire at a mysterious roadblock in Mexico, a nation whose culture has been labeled by some as the birthplace of strident machismo. Clarke's precocious critique noted:

> There are millions of gays, however, and millions of straights too who live out their lives without bothering to bow to *butchness*. One of the truly great and lasting effects of the

hippie ethic was its exposure and its attempted destruction of outworn masculinism. Unisex clothing, long hair for men, abandoning makeup for women, beads, bells, and hair-flowers, all made clear the hip philosophy that people are people and that to relate to human beings as "men," women," "straight," and "gay" is to cut them into strict confining patterns. . . . A truly complete person is neither extremely masculine nor extremely feminine. There is a balance of the various elements and a free interplay. . . . It is high time that American men learned that there is nothing sissified about poetry, nothing "faggy" about great music, and nothing queer about deep emotions. . . . Our ultimate masculine gods are those of aggression. . . . We must learn that they are false gods, shadows to which we bow in ignorance. Why are we kneeling before them? They have no feelings, no tenderness, no thoughts or sensitivity. Why have we chosen such gods? Because Americans are desperately and needlessly afraid. What a shame. Its citizens fear that they will be thought homosexually inclined.[5]

Unfortunately, today little attention is given to male roles beyond conformist jargon made stricter by fundamentalist religious taboos. If the heterosexually inclined male understands that he, too, can play a revolutionary part, he takes his place on the cutting edge of change, becoming aware of the unnecessary sufferings of subjugated women and conscious of the limitations of his own prescribed role. He also becomes free from the fear of showing his deepest feelings, conscious of the heightened awareness and beauty an androgynous psychology brings him, removing the heavy chains he fastens on himself if he perpetuates the anti-homosexual taboo. With his face turned confidently toward the future, he leaves behind his reactionary status as the brunt of feminist hostility, becoming a co-participant in the birthing of a new world.

NOTES

1. Robert Burns, *Poems and Songs of Robert Burns,* ed. James Barke (London and Glasgow: Collins, 1953), p. 643.

2. James A. Doyles, *The Male Experience* (Dubuque, Iowa: Wm. C. Brown Co., 1983), p. 289.

3. Melinda Henneberger with Michel Marriott, "For Some, Abuse Replaces Youthful Courtship," *New York Times,* July 11, 1993, section 1, p. 1.

4. Robert Gould, Professor of Psychiatry, New York Medical College.

5. Lige Clarke and Jack Nichols, "He-Man Horseshit," in the "Homosexual Citizen" column, *SCREW,* May 23, 1969.

Sexual Integration

*One cannot classify homosexual and heterosexual tendencies as
being mutually exclusive or even opposed to each other.*
> Clellan S. Ford and Frank A. Beach,
> *Patterns of Sexual Behavior*[1]

IF HUMAN BEINGS are born with bisexual potential, which they
are, according to psychological assessments already described, the question remains as to why fewer people openly
express themselves homosexually. I contend that it is partly
because humanity, like its primate cousins, is imitative: *monkey
see, monkey do.* Cultural propagandists, given over to a shameless promoting of one-sided heterosexual behavior, are aware
that only a strong taboo will keep homosexuality at bay. Heterosexual supremacists, taking their original cues from religious dogmas, have heretofore kept those urges tightly repressed with the assistance of legal penalties, religious guide-
lines, and social stigmas. The religious fundamentalists'
agenda includes an unprecedented strengthening of their
hear-nothing, see-nothing, speak-nothing repression. If mon-

keys can't see, they won't do, goes their taboo-riddled reasoning.

On its way toward the promised land of social liberty, the gay liberation movement itself has gone through important stages of self-identification, including the addition of lesbian and bisexual categories. Lesbian issues and concerns, as noted previously, differ markedly from those of males, while bisexuals have been subjected to thoughtless prejudices lobbed from both sides of the sexual continuum. Now, however, the movement's more official name rightly encompasses gay men, lesbians, and bisexuals. Bisexuals, finally, have a say.

According to the statistics of the Kinsey report, which describe the sexual behavior of men:

> Males do not represent two discrete populations, heterosexual and homosexual. The world is not to be divided into sheep and goats. Not all things are black nor all things white. It is a fundamental of taxonomy that nature rarely deals with discrete categories. Only the human mind invents categories and tries to force facts into separated pigeon holes. The living world is a continuum in each and every one of its aspects. The sooner we learn this about human sexual behavior, the sooner we shall reach a sound understanding of the realities of sex.[2]

Theories about homosexual behavior have continued, since the last century, to divide expert researchers. One faction, the psychobiologists, posits a kind of "third sex" doctrine, claiming that homosexual conduct has its roots in biological fiats. In 1991 Simon LeVay, a gay genetic researcher, advanced certain biological essentialist claims about the brain matter of gay males, basing his statements on the studies on nineteen men who had died of AIDS. The male heterosexual's hypothalamus, he said, is larger than that of gay males. No comparable studies were conducted among women. A number of gay activists, unfamiliar with the extended struggle between psychobiology and social constructionist psychology, rushed to assert that homosexuality is inborn. Hoping to quell fundamentalist charges that homosexuals deliberately choose their orientations, and are, therefore, immoral, these activists have sought to show that choice about such matters is nonexistent, that homosexual inclinations are genetically produced and are therefore nature's decree.

Their approach, unfortunately, unwittingly retains homosexuality's boxed-in status, making of gay men and lesbians a group set apart from others by genetics, a fixed minority. Unless a genetic predisposition to bisexuality can also be proved, this approach does little to address society's evolving recognition of bisexuals, a group once thought to be either self-deceiving or nonexistent. In fact, bisexual inclinations are far more widespread than has previously been thought, and a host of celebrities have proclaimed bisexual leanings. Among the earliest was the famed German-born actress Marlene Dietrich, who, according to her daughter's detailed accounts, had passionate affairs with both sexes.[3] In her wake, male stars like Marlon Brando have spoken publicly about their same-sex trysts. "Like a large number of men," said Brando, "I have had homosexual experiences and I am not ashamed. Homosexuality is so much in fashion, it no longer makes news."[4]

Those who would denigrate bisexuality, however, say that there is a difference between homosexuals and bisexuals in that the latter generally lean emotionally toward one sex or the other, thus retaining only two strict categories, gay and straight. In cases such as Dietrich's or Brando's, they would point to marriages to prove this contention, though many bisexuals insist that it is the quality of a relationship that counts rather than the sex of a partner. My own observations have led me to believe that bisexuality—signaling the opening up of options—is now just entering upon the stage of our evolving human consciousness; that choice is based, mostly unconsciously, on social values; and that the newly revived genetic arguments of the biological essentialists are simply another weary round in an ongoing century-long battle between biological essentialism and social constructionism.* If the unlikely genetic argument were to prove unassailable, however, gay activists, on the one hand, and anti-abortionists, on the other, would bypass each other as each group fled to opposite corners. Fundamentalists, discovering gay genes during routine examinations of each fetus, would opt for abortions. Pat Robertson, Jerry Falwell, D. James Kennedy, and others would beg hasty admission to the very clinics they now oppose. Gay, lesbian, and bisexual activists, on the other hand, would find themselves marching against selective abortions sought only because of perceived homosexual genes.

I myself am a social constructionist. My reasons for this are not unlike those of feminists who deny, as I do, that anatomy is destiny, an argument used *ad nauseam* to deny women equal rights. To speak of destiny in this fashion, I contend, is to deny humankind its potential to make needed evolutionary changes, an elasticity that is basic to its welfare. Part of that welfare, as I see it, now involves a reduction in world population, a goal to which a marked increase in homosexual relations contributes.

The heterosexually inclined psychotherapist Dr. George

---

*"It appears that their [social constructionists'] most basic tenet is that what has been popularly regarded as a fixed biological reality is malleable." (from *If You Seduce a Straight Person, Can You Make Them Gay?* ed. John P. DeCecco and John P. Elia)[5]

Weinberg, coiner of the word "homophobia" and author of *Society and the Healthy Homosexual,* insists that Simon LeVay and his school of biological essentialists are forever trying to reassert "scientific" dominion over human behavioral patterns. Psychobiological binges, he says, erupt somewhat regularly and get front-page coverage. Afterward they fade again into the backdrop of our collective memory, moving into a limbo of perpetual nonimportance. "These theories," says Dr. Weinberg, "will be propounded as long as dull citizens want to explain human differences rather than celebrate them."[6]

Most sexologists, including Kinsey, Pomeroy, and Martin, insist that sexual behaviors are not instinctual but are learned. No infinitesimal section of the cerebrum can be dissected and said to produce, by itself, the kaleidoscopic fantasia which reaches outward to encompass the entirety of our sexual perspective. LeVay and company can dance across all body parts in their possession with enthusiasm, but their findings will have no more significance than those of primitive psychics who use animal entrails to tell the future.

What, then, *is* homosexuality? It is one side of the sexual continuum. This answer was reached after the publication of the 1948 Kinsey studies which said that 37.5 percent of all males (straight or gay) reach at least one orgasm homosexually in adulthood. Up to 50 percent fantasize same-sex relations, though social condemnation keeps them from acting on these fantasies. A more recent study (1994), conducted by researchers at the Harvard School of Public Health, finds that one in every five persons could be considered "incidentally homosexual," because of homosexual desire or behavior experienced after age fifteen. "Our perspective," said David Wypij, a co-author of the study, "is that sexual orientation isn't just a yes-no, heterosexual-homosexual [question]."[7] Thus, in terms of potential, homosexuality can no longer be consid-

ered statistically insignificant. The higher percentage of inci-
dental male homosexuality found in the 1994 study suggests
that the number of males so inclined may, because of public
awareness, have increased since 1948.

Among other anomalies with which sexologists are well
acquainted, is the fact that the most common heterosexual
male fantasy is to watch women performing homosexually. Kinsey's fifty-year-old statistics about female homosexual behavior
indicated that there were fewer lesbians, although in the intervening decades, same-sex love among women—particularly
since the advent of 1960s feminism—has greatly increased; so
much so, in fact, that lesbian social life now rivals, in many
locales, that formerly enjoyed only by gay men. The reason? A
throwing off by women of repressive constraints, namely, those
discouraging expressive sexual behaviors.

In the late 1960s, under the influence of LSD, a significant
number of heterosexually inclined men experienced what was
called "homosexual panic." Looking deep into their own psy-
ches, many found, not surprisingly, that male bodies like their
own were proving attractive. Conversely, gay men, under the
same drug, often found women appealing. Under the influence of LSD, they placed less significance on specific body
parts, or what might be called a previously heightened ana-
tomical overfocus, and found enjoyment instead in a general
suffusion of erotic feelings through human tactile contact.

Mart Crowley's well-known play, *The Boys in the Band,* has a
leading character, Michael, discussing how many men, while
keeping to their heterosexual identities, engage, nevertheless,
in the "Christ-was-I-drunk-last-night syndrome." He explains
how a man often "makes it" with "some guy in school and the
next day when you had to face each other there was always a
lot of shit-kicking crap about, 'Man, was I drunk last night!
Christ, I don't remember a thing.' "[8]

That straight-identified men or women often behave homosexually is, to many, no surprise. Arrest statistics compiled by police decoys conducting entrapments in public parks and other locales that allow anonymity, show that a large majority of those arrested are married. This shows, I believe, that there is diminishing significance in being labeled or categorized sexually as homosexual or heterosexual, and that many already approach their emotional and sexual experiences outside these labels. Since sexuality is a learning process, some have realized that sex has wider perimeters, that gender must not necessarily be specific to ensure satisfaction. They sense that sexual preferences are, to a great degree, learned. In fact, bisexuals may decry such preferences, wondering why somebody can only enjoy partners who are blondes, or younger people, or older people. These preferences may be regarded as inhibitions. Touch and sensitivity take place between personalities as well as anatomies, and many men and women resist limitations based on gender.

If women's liberation has opened the door to same-sex love among females, only a movement questioning the gender system as it still adversely affects men will do likewise among males.[9] Anthropology and historical records prove that whole societies have incorporated homosexuality as a natural phenomenon. Other historical trends, especially those associated with earlier epochs, have promoted heterosexism to foster tribe growth. But love among men and among women was long ago widespread in Greece and Rome, prevalent until the advent of the conquering Judaeo-Christian traditions.

Human groupings must see their various futures as inclusive of each other rather than exclusive. *No man is an island.* Looked at from this all-encompassing angle, homosexual or heterosexual relations become the natural birthright of every man and woman. Early conditioning—especially what primates are allowed to *see*—presently sends most hurrying toward the overcrowded heterosexual side of the continuum. The taboos taught keep a respectable percentage from claiming same-sex love as a birthright, thus cutting in half their potential for the enjoyment of all available human contact. This is, to my mind, unfortunate.

What can be done? The answer lies delightfully curled like a sleeping baby within the cradle of equal rights. These rights point not only to such matters as employment and housing, but they go much farther, squarely into that still-forbidden domain: free expression. I, for one, believe that the fundamentalist fear of "the prairie fire effect," namely, that unchecked homosexuality will spread far and wide, is quite on target. Instinctively, they know as I do about man's imitative capacities. The most radical dimension of the gay, lesbian, and bisexual movement, then, revolves around a word which heterosexual supremacists use pejoratively to describe their disgust. That word is *flaunting*. To flaunt, from this standpoint, is to hold hands publicly, to kiss at a bus stop, to make clear, in other words, while others are within eyeshot, that homosexual love is composed of all those affectionate or passionate features that have made heterosexuality so alluring. Why are these behaviors tabooed? Because fundamentalists fear the truth of *monkey see, monkey do*.

It is time now to call for equal treatment in every social dimension. The publishing industry, fortunately, is catching up with this idea. Gay, lesbian, and bisexual studies are mushrooming in academic spheres. But news media, advertising and TV networks remain somewhat squeamish, and though there have been a variety of films with gay themes, much remains to be done not only to integrate realistic heterosexual, homosexual, and bisexual characters into everyday encounters, but to invest them with an equal measure of affectionate contact.

In advertising, too, there needs to be integration. That markets aimed at a vast same-sex constituency must confine themselves to gay media alone is ludicrous. There are subtle changes now in progress, but these must expand rapidly, simply to guarantee that markets reach sizable segments of the population whom—to their own detriment—they now ignore. There must be explicit photographs celebrating same-sex comradeship, just as heterosexuality is celebrated. If blue-noses object, let them. Bigots once objected to portrayals of other groups comprising varied parts of the American dream, but their boiling points soon cooled to a simmer and the controversies surrounding such portrayals faded.

Let those who find such proposals "radical," examine, without haste, the status quo and what it portends for the future. There is no current evidence that heterosexuality is the mark of a superior race. By the year 2035, if present demographics continue, heterosexual supremacists who are resisting, quelling, subduing, repressing, and restraining every natural homosexual component in their own and others' otherwise diffident personalities, will have doubled the number of people on the earth. While they worry unnecessarily about openly gay scoutmasters, heterosexual offspring will be dying of starvation and malnutrition at the rate of a half million per week.

The fundamentalist fear that homosexuals are out to "recruit" is hardly fair. Heterosexuals recruit without giving it a second thought. Heterosexuals *flaunt* all the time, flashing photos of their pinups, their mates, and their offspring. Heterosexual romantic trysts are dominant subjects in nearly every cultural climate. It is high time that homosexual relations get equal billing. Do heterosexuals fear there will be competition? Do they think homosexual equality spells the end of heterosexuality itself? Are they so insecure? I should

204 ▼ THE GAY AGENDA

hope not. As Roslyn Regelson, an instructor at New York University who was the first to teach a course on gay studies, said, "Heterosexuality will always hold its own on the marketplace."[10]

It remains for thoughtful people of all persuasions to destroy each perverted fence that has been erected to prevent same-sex love because of fundamentalist hate mongering. If this is not done with great rapidity on a wide scale, humanity's natural sympathies, deformed and prohibited by biases against sex and the body, will be transformed into frustrations that will burst on us in waves of hostile reverberation. Alan Watts, the great Zen Buddhist scholar, makes a cogent point when he writes:

> If... young and unrealized homosexuals who affect machismo, ultramasculinity, and who constitute the hard core of our military industrial police Mafia combine would go fuck each other (and I use that word in its most appreciative and loving sense), the world would be vastly improved. They make it with women only to brag about it, but are actually far happier in the barracks than in boudoirs. This is, perhaps, the real meaning of "Make Love, Not War." We may be destroying ourselves through the repression of homosexuality.

In his brilliant autobiography, *In My Own Way,* Watts suggested that a heaven in which he lies (as the old hymn says) "forever on my Savior's breast," might be fun for nuns, "but for a man it is the invitation to the boredom of a homosexual paradise." "This is not to say," he assures us, "that I condemn homosexuality, but only that I do not enjoy it."[11]

Machismo stifles natural human sympathies, affecting relations with either sex. Men might reach out to embrace other men, but the staid voice of what they are pleased to call masculine etiquette reminds them that occasions for affectionate squeezes should be few and far between. Such squeezes, they are taught, are improper. Men shake hands instead, a custom deriving from ancient times, purportedly to show they are carrying no weapons.

"In the past," lamented the anthropologist Margaret Mead, "society was very destructive to any male friendship. It was always expressed by that terrible bang on the back." Mead knew that men, because of cultural conditioning, find it difficult to admit to themselves that each has within himself the capability of responding in various ways and at surprising times to either sex. She realized, as Kinsey showed, that a majority of men wish for fulfillment, at one time or another, with another male, a wish that is strongly suppressed by the dominant culture. Mead writes: "It is possible to distort the upbringing of every male so that his capacity and temptation to introduce sex into his relationship with other males is very strong and yet kept closely in control."[12]

This, does not mean, however that the men Mead describes are exclusive homosexuals. It means simply that the human mind and body are esthetically attractive on occasion and that neither heterosexuality nor homosexuality is an exclusive state of being. Friendship has no particular relationship to homosexuality per se, but the fear of being thought gay has, tragically, prevented passionate and intimate same-sex friendships from blooming, except, of course, among the gay-identified "minority" which has banded together to defend its right to have such relationships.

If homosexually inclined American men and women have led the battle to open our way to expressing love to members of our own sex, then heterosexually inclined people must help us finish that battle. Otherwise, the worldwide comradeship of which the poets sing will never have a chance. As Margaret

Mead points out, affection has been perversely distorted be-
N3 cause of cultural conditioning. In America this has been
brought about principally because of interfering dogmatic
religionists. Fundamentalists are now engaged in a life-and-
death battle to retain this distortion.

Robert Burns, whose poetry happily celebrates heterosexual passions, looked forward, nevertheless, to a future when
"man to man, the world o'er shall brithers be," and it is important for planetary survival that other heterosexually inclined
men share this vision, that they can be free to hug or touch a
friend and that nobody will think the unthinkable. Burns led
the way when he wrote of his lifelong friendship with John
Anderson:

> *John Anderson my jo, John,*
> *When we were first acquent* [acquainted]
> *Your locks were like the raven,*
> *Your bonnie brow was brent* [straight];
> *But now your brow is beld* [bald], *John,*
> *Your locks are like the snaw,*
> *But blessings on your frosty pow* [pate],
> *John Anderson my jo!*

> *John Anderson my jo, John,*
> *We clamb* [climbed] *the hill thegither* [together];
> *And mony* [many] *a cantie* [jolly] *day, John,*
> *We've had wi' ane anither* [one another]:
> *Now we maun* [must] *totter down, John,*
> *And hand in hand we'll go*
> *And sleep thegither at the foot,*
> *John Anderson, my jo.*[13]

And even if another *does* think the unthinkable, it won't matter because (1) it isn't true; (2) it doesn't matter what other people think; and (3) a human ought to understand that affection, whether homosexual or heterosexual, is highly preferable to its lack. In all areas it needs encouragement as an antidote to hostility. Walt Whitman sang:

> *Over the carnage rose prophetic a voice,*
> *Be not disheartn'd, affection shall solve the*
> *problems of freedom yet.*[14]

What did Whitman mean? Certainly not that genital contact alone could soothe the human condition. But affection, yes, or even love. "Love one another," said Jesus, "as I have loved you." Why, it must be asked, was it acceptable for Jesus to kiss his male friends, and why is such a practice not acceptable in nations where his so-called followers roam? Ask the fundamentalists. They know everything there is to know about truth.

NOTES

1. Clellan S. Ford and Frank A. Beach, *Patterns of Sexual Behavior* (New York: Harper & Row, 1951).

2. Alfred C. Kinsey, Wardell B. Pomeroy, and Clyde E. Martin, *Sexual Behavior in the Human Male* (Philadelphia: W. B. Saunders, 1948), p. 639.

3. Maria Riva, *Dietrich* (New York, Alfred A. Knopf, 1993).

4. Marlon Brando quoted in *Long Road to Freedom: The Advocate History of the Gay and Lesbian Movement* (New York: St. Martin's Press, 1994), p. 130.

5. John P. DeCecco and John P. Elia, eds., "Introduction," *If You Seduce a Straight Person, Can You Make Him Gay?* (Binghamton, N.Y.: Harrington Park Press, 1993), p. 4.

6. George Weinberg, Ph.D., in an interview with the author, October 1991.

7. Associated Press, "Study Examines Homosexual Feelings: 1 in 5 Americans Have Been Attracted to Same Sex," *Florida Today*, September 6, 1994, p. 4–A.

8. Mart Crowley, quoted in *Unnatural Quotations*, ed. Leigh W. Rutledge (Boston: Alyson Publications, 1988), p. 32.

9. Jack Nichols, *Men's Liberation: A New Definition of Masculinity* (New York: Penguin Books, 1975).

10. Eleanor Lester, "The First Professor of Homosexuality," *GAY*, February 15, 1971, p. 5.

11. Alan Watts, *In My Own Way* (New York: Vintage Books, 1973), p. 42.

12. Dr. Margaret Mead, *Male and Female* (Hammondsworth, England: Penguin Books, Ltd., 1950).

13. Robert Burns, *Poems and Songs of Robert Burns*, ed. James Barke (Glasgow and London: Collins, 1962), p. 510.

14. Walt Whitman, *Leaves of Grass* (Amherst N. Y.: Prometheus Books, 1995).

References and Bibliography

Alderman, Ellen, and Caroline Kennedy. *The Right to Privacy.* New York: Alfred A. Knopf, 1995.

Alexander, Kathey, and Gail White. "Focus on American Vision: Christian Reconstructionists Advance a Radical Christian Belief That Includes Support for Cobb's Anti-Gay Resolution." *Atlanta Constitution,* July 5, 1994, p. B–5.

Allport, Gordon. *The Nature of Prejudice.* Reading, Mass.: Addison Wesley, 1954.

Alwood, Edward. *Straight News: Gays, Lesbians and the Media.* New York: Columbia University Press, 1996.

"AIDS Ruckus in the Vatican." *Time,* November 27, 1989, p. 58.

Anchell, Melvin. Interview with John F. McManus, "Unsafe in Any Grade." *The New American,* May 11, 1987, p. A–1.

Ardery, Robert. *The Territorial Imperative: A Personal Inquiry into the Animal Origins of Property and Nations.* New York: Dell Publishing Co., Inc., 1971.

Associated Press. "Anti-Semitism Report Is a Hot Potato for Vatican." *Miami Herald,* May 27, 1994, p. 17–A.

———. "Ecologist: Population Must Drop to 2 Billion." *Florida Today,* February 22, 1994, p. 4-A.

Associated Press. "Low AIDS Budget of F.D.A. Said to Slow Drug Approval." *New York Times,* February 20, 1988.

———. "Study Examines Homosexual Feelings: 1 in 5 Americans Have Been Attracted to the Same Sex." *Florida Today,* September 6, 1994, p. 4-A.

———. "Waxman: Reagan Failing on AIDS." August 10, 1986.

Badie, Rick. "Lake Schoolboard Chairwoman Tries to Limit Gay, Multicultural Education." *Orlando Sentinel,* June 11, 1993, p. B–1.

Baker, Chris. "Heterosexuality on the Rampage." *Baltimore Alternative,* February 1996, p. 3.

Baker, Roger. *Drag: A History of Female Impersonation in the Performing Arts.* New York: New York University Press, 1994.

Bailey, Derrick Sherwin. *Homosexuality and the Western Christian Tradition.* New York: Longmans, Green, 1955.

Bakunin, Michael. *God and the State.* New York: Dover Publications, Inc., 1970.

Beauvoir, Simone de. *The Second Sex,* ed. and trans. H. M. Parshley. New York: Alfred A. Knopf, Inc., 1953.

Bergman, Lewis. "Perspectives on Provincetown." *New York Times,* July 17, 1983, section 10, p. 14.

Bernstein, Robert A. *Straight Parents Gay Children: Keeping Families Together.* New York: Thunder's Mouth Press, 1995.

Berreby, David. "I'm The Anti-Family Voter." *New York Times,* August 29, 1992, section 1, p. 19.

Boffey, Philip M. "AIDS Panel Chief Urges Ban on Bias against Infected." *New York Times,* June 3, 1988, p. A–1.

———. "Expert Panel Sees Poor Leadership in U.S. AIDS Battle." *New York Times,* June 2, 1988, p. 1.

———. "FDA Budget for AIDS Called Too Low." *New York Times,* February 20, 1988, p. A–9.

———. "Health Officials Fault U.S. Response to AIDS Epidemic." *New York Times,* August 13, 1987, p. A–20.

Bono, Edward de. *Handbook for the Positive Revolution.* New York: Penguin Books, 1992.

Boston, Robert. *The Most Dangerous Man in America? Pat Robertson and the Rise of the Christian Coalition.* Amherst: N.Y.: Prometheus Books, 1996.

Brenton, Myron. *The American Male.* New York: Fawcett World Library, 1966.

Brown, Lester. "Natural Limits." *New York Times,* July 94 ·993, section 1, p. 19.

Burkett, Elinor. *The Gravest Show on Earth.* Boston: Houghton Mifflin Co. 1995.

Burns, Robert. *Poems and Songs of Robert Burns,* ed. James Barke. London and Glasgow: Collins, 1953.

Byron, Lord (George Gordon). "Don Juan," 1821. In *The Great Thoughts,* ed. George Seldes. New York: Ballantine Books, 1985, p. 63.

Callahan, Nathan, and William Payton, eds. *Shut Up Fag! Quotations from the Files of Congressman Bob Dornan, The Man Who Would Be President.* Irvine Calif.: Mainstreet Media, 1994.

Cantwell, Dr. Alan, Jr. *Queer Blood: The Secret AIDS Genocide Plot.* Los Angeles: Aries Rising Press, 1993.

Carpenter, Edward. *The Healing of Nations and the Hidden Sources of Their Strife.* London: George Allen and Unwin, Ltd., 1915.

———. "The Intermediate Sex." In *Selected Writings,* vol. 1, *Sex.* London: Gay Men's Press, 1984.

———. "Love's Coming of Age." In *Selected Writings,* vol. 1, *Sex.* London: Gay Men's Press, 1984.

———. *My Days and Dreams.* London: George Allen and Unwin, Ltd., 1916.

———. *Pagan and Christian Creeds: Their Origin and Meaning.* New York: Harcourt, Brace and Co., 1920.

———. *Towards Democracy.* London: T. Fisher Unwin, 1892.

Carpenter, Edward, ed. *Iolaus: An Anthology of Friendship.* New York: Pagan Press, 1982.

Chari, V. K. *Whitman in the Light of Vedantic Mysticism.* Lincoln: University of Nebraska Press, 1964.

Chauncey, George. *Gay New York: Gender, Urban Culture and the Making of the Gay Male World, 1890–1940.* New York: Basic Books, 1994.

Chua-Edan, Howard. "After The Fall: Faced with lawsuits and struggling to treat clerics accused of sexual abuse, the Catholic Church lags behind in forging a policy on priestly pedophilia." *Time*, May 9, 1994, p. 56.

Churchill, Wainwright. *Homosexual Behavior among Males: A Cross-Cultural and Cross-Species Investigation.* Alexandria, Va.: Hawthorn Books, 1967.

Clarity, James F. "Catholic Church in Ireland Faces Sex Scandals." *New York Times,* October 19, 1995, p. A–7.

Clarke, Lige, and Jack Nichols. "He-Man Horseshit." Homosexual Citizen column, *SCREW,* May 23, 1969.

———. *I Have More Fun with You Than Anybody.* New York: St. Martin's Press, 1972; London: St. James Press, 1976.

———. *Roommates Can't Always Be Lovers: An Intimate Guide to Male/Male Relationships.* New York: St. Martin's Press, 1974; London: St. James Press, 1976.

Cooper, Dr. David. *The Death of the Family.* New York: Random House, 1971.

Coote, Stephen, ed. *The Penguin Book of Homosexual Verse.* New York: Penguin Books, 1983.

Cory, Donald Webster. *The Homosexual in America.* New York: Greenberg, 1951.

Cory, Donald Webster, ed. *Homosexuality: A Cross-Cultural Approach.* New York: Julian Press, 1956.

Cowell, Alan. "Legendary Big Italian Family Becoming Thing of the Past." *New York Times,* August 28, 1993, p. A–1.

———. "Vatican Attacks Population Stand Supported by U.S., Abortion and Homosexuality Are Seen as Major Issues at Talks in September." *New York Times,* August 9, 1994, p. A–1.

———. "Vatican Fights U.N. Draft on Women's Rights." *New York Times,* June 15, 1994, p. A–1.

"Curriculum Fight, An Unlikely Catalyst." *New York Times,* November 27, 1992, p. B–1.

The Dhammapada, trans. P. Lal. New York: Farrar, Straus and Giroux, Inc., 1967.

Davies, Bon. "Will We Offer Hope?" *MOODY*, May 1994, p. 12.

D'Emilio, John. *Sexual Politics/Sexual Communities: The Making of a Homosexual Minority in the United States (1940–1970).* Chicago: University of Chicago Press, 1983.

"Desecrating Yad Veshem." *Jerusalem Post,* June 1, 1994, p. 6.

DeWitt, Karen. "Basketball on Capital Hill, The Battle for AIDS Funds Heats Up." *New York Times,* November 9, 1991, section 1, p. 33.

Doyle, James A. *The Male Experience.* Dubuque, Iowa: William C. Brown Co., 1984.

Due, Linnea. *Joining the Tribe: Growing Up Gay and Lesbian in the 90's.* New York: Anchor Books, Doubleday, 1995.

Ellman, Richard, ed. *The Artist as Critic.* New York: Random House, 1968.

Emerson, Ralph Waldo. *The Complete Essays and Other Writings of Ralph Waldo Emerson.* New York: Modern Library College Editions, 1953.

"Enter the AIDS Pandemic: The Experts Predict that 100 Million Will Be Stricken by 1990." *Time,* December 1, 1986, p. 45.

Epstein, Joseph. "Homo-Hetero: The Struggle for Sexual Identity." *Harper's,* September 1970, p. 51.

Falwell, Jerry. Speech delivered in *Thy Kingdom Come,* a film by Antony Thomas, 1988.

Farrell, Warren. *The Liberated Man, Beyond Masculinity: Freeing Men and Their Relationships with Women.* New York: Random House, 1975.

Ferenz, George. "Gay Movement Earns Milestone Legal Victory." *Florida's Hot Spots,* Memorial Day Issue, 1996, p. 58.

Fernbach, David. *The Spiral Path: A Gay Contribution to Human Survival.* London: The Gay Men's Press, 1981.

Fox, Thomas C. *Sexuality and Catholicism.* New York: George Braziller, Inc., 1995.

Frank, Waldo. *The Rediscovery of America.* New York: Duell-Sloan, Piarce, 1929.

———. *The Rediscovery of Man: A Memoir and a Methodology of Modern Life.* New York: George Braziller, Inc., 1958.

Frank, Waldo. *Salvos.* New York: Boni & Liveright, Inc., 1924.

Franklin, Benjamin. *Writings.* New York: The Library of America, Library of Classics of the United States, 1987.

Funny Gay Males. *Growing Up Gay: From Left Out to Coming Out.* New York: Hyperion, 1995.

Garber, Marjorie. *Vice Versa: Bisexuality and the Eroticism of Everyday Life.* New York: Simon and Schuster, 1995.

Gentry, Carol. "In Sarasota, Koop Honors Three for Fighting AIDS Prejudice." *St. Petersburg Times,* April 11, 1989, p. 1–A.

Gerzon, Mark. *A Choice of Heroes: The Changing Face of American Manhood.* Boston: Houghton Mifflin Co., 1982.

√ Gibran, Kahlil. *The Prophet.* New York: Alfred A. Knopf, Inc., 1923.

Glazer, Nathan, and David Reisman. "The Intellectuals and the Discontented Classes." *Faces in the Crowd.* New York: Arno Press, 1979.

√ Goff, Michael, and the staff of *OUT* magazine. *Out in America, A Portrait of Gay and Lesbian Life.* New York: Penguin-Viking, 1994.

Goodman, Paul. *Growing Up Absurd.* New York: Alfred K. Knopf, 1956.

Gould, Dr. Robert E. Oberlin College Conference: "Snakes and Snails and Puppydog Tails: Why Shouldn't Men Be Gentle, Caring, Loving Sharing," October 19, 1973.

Greenberg, David F. *The Construction of Homosexuality.* Chicago: The University of Chicago Press, 1988.

Hallen, S. "If Papa Won't Preach It, Young Ron Reagan Will, with a TV Pitch Promoting Safe Sex." *People,* July 13, 1987, pp. 38–40.

Heron, A. *Toward a Quaker View of Sex.* London: Friends Home Service Committee, 1963.

Henneberger, Melinda, and Michel Marriott. "For Some, Abuse Replaces Youthful Courtship." *New York Times,* July 11, 1993, section 1, p. 1.

Hoffer, Eric. *The True Believer.* New York: Harper & Row, 1951.

Holt, Rackham. "Margaret Higgins Sanger." *Collier's Encyclopedia,* London and New York: P. F. Collier, Inc., vol. 20, 1978, p. 403.

Homel, Steven H. *The Competition Obsession: A Philosophy of Non-Competitive Living.* San Diego: ACS Publishing Co., 1981.

Hoult, Thomas Ford, Lura F. Menze, and John W. Hudson. *Courtship and Marriage in America.* Boston: Little, Brown & Co., 1978.

Hunter, John Francis (John Paul Hudson). *The Gay Insider U.S.A.* New York: Stonehill Publications, 1972.

Ingersoll, Robert G. *The Best of Ingersoll: Selections from His Writings and Speeches,* ed. Roger E. Greeley. Amherst, N.Y.: Prometheus Books, 1983.

————. *Reason, Tolerance and Christianity, The Ingersoll Debates.* Amherst, N.Y.: Prometheus Books, 1993.

————. *Some Mistakes of Moses.* Amherst, N.Y.: Prometheus Books, 1986.

Israel, Constance Denney. *Hate Crimes against Gays/Lesbians.* Los Colinas, Tex.: Monument Press, 1992.

Isherwood, Christopher. *My Guru and His Disciple.* New York: Farrar, Straus and Giroux, 1980.

Isikoff, Michael. "Evangelists Defend Funding Tactics: Decry House Hearings As Dangerous Precedent." *Washington Post,* October 7, 1987, p. C–1.

Jay, Karla, ed. *Lesbian Erotica.* New York and London: New York University Press, 1995.

Jefferson, Thomas. *The Life and Selected Writings of Thomas Jefferson,* ed. Adrian Koch and William Peden. New York: Modern Library, Random House, 1944.

Johnson, David K. "Homosexual Citizens." *Washington History,* Fall/Winter 1994–1995.

Jones, Julia Runk, and Milo Trump. *Livingston's Field Guide to North American Males.* Garden City, N.Y.: Doubleday, 1984.

Kameny, Franklin E., Ph.D. "Amending District of Columbia Charitable Solicitation Act." Transcript of hearing by House of Representatives Subcommittee No. 4 on the Committee on the District of Columbia HR5990, Thursday, August 8, 1963.

Katz, Jonathan Ned. *The Invention of Heterosexuality.* New York: Dutton, 1995.

King, Florence. *Confessions of a Failed Southern Lady.* New York: St. Martin's Press, 1985.

King, Florence. *Southern Ladies and Gentlemen*. New York: Stein and Day, 1975.

Kinsey, Alfred C., Wardell B. Pomeroy and Clyde E. Martin. *Sexual Behavior in the Human Male*. Philadelphia: W. B. Saunders, 1948.

Kirshner, Alan M. *Masculinity in an Historical Perspective: Readings and Discussions*. Washington, D.C.: University Press of America, 1977.

Kropotkin, Peter. *The Essential Kropotkin: A General Selection from the Writings of the Great Russian Anarchist Thinker*, eds. Emile Capouvya and Keitha Tompkins. New York: Liveright, 1975.

Lader, Lawrence. *Breeding Ourselves to Death*. New York: Ballatine Books, 1971.

Leitsch, Dick. "Gay Lore's Heroes and Bores." *GAY*, August, 1973.

Lester, Eleanor. "Professor of Homosexuality." *GAY*, February 15, 1971, p. 5.

Levine, Martin P. *Gay Men: The Sociology of Male Homosexuality*. New York: Harper & Row, 1979.

Lewis, Anthony. "What Will Happen." *New York Times*, February 19, 1993.

Linden, Robin Ruth, Darlene R. Pagano, Diana E. H. Russell, and Susan Leigh Star, eds. *Against Sadomasochism: A Radical Feminist Analysis*. San Francisco: Frog in the Well, 1982.

Lorenz, Konrad. *On Aggression*, trans. Majorie K. Wilson. New York: Bantam Books, Inc., 1970.

McFarland, Norman F. Excerpt from July 1993 issue of the diocesan newspaper *The Bulletin*. In *Miami Herald*, August 2, 1993, Op. Ed.

McWilliams, Peter. *Ain't Nobody's Business If You Do: The Absurdity of Consensual Crimes in a Free Society*. Los Angeles: Prelude Press, 1993.

Marcus, Eric. *Is It a Choice?* San Francisco: HarperCollins, 1993.

Martello, Leo Louis. *Weird Ways of Witchcraft*. New York: H. C. Publishers, Inc., 1969.

Martin, Robert K. *The Homosexual Tradition in American Poetry*. Austin and London: The University of Texas Press, 1979.

Marwick, Charles. "Health and Justice Professionals Set Goals to Lessen Domestic Violence." *Journal of the American Medical Association* 27, no. 15 (April 20, 1994): 1147.

Mead, Margaret. *Male and Female.* Hammondsworth, England: Penguin Books, Ltd., 1950.

"Memo Urges Justice Department to Polarize Debate on Key Issues." *New York Times,* February 24, 1988.

Mencken, H. L. "Memorial Service." In *Prejudices: A Selection.* New York: Vintage Books, 1958.

————. *A Mencken Chrestomathy: His Own Selection of His Choicest Writings.* New York: Alfred A. Knopf, 1949.

Miller, James E., Jr., Karl Shapiro, and Bernice Slote. *Start with the Sun: Studies in the Whitman Tradition.* Lincoln: University of Nebraska Press, 1960.

✓ Miller, Neil. *Out of the Past: Gay and Lesbian History from 1869 to the Present.* New York: Vintage Books, 1995.

Mishima, Yukio. *Confessions of a Mask.* New York: New Directions, 1958 (1949).

✓ Monette, Paul. *Becoming a Man.* New York: Harcourt, Brace Jovanovich, Inc., 1992.

Montagu, Ashley. *The American Way of Life.* New York: G. P. Putnam's Sons, 1967.

————, ed. *Man and Aggression.* New York: Oxford University Press, 1968.

Monteagudo, Jesse. "Books and Gay Identity: A Personal Look." In *Gay Life: Leisure, Love and Living for the Contemporary Gay Male,* ed. Eric Rofes. Garden City, N.Y.: Doubleday, 1986.

Montessori, Maria. *Il Bambino in famiglia.* Milan: Gazenti Editore, 1956.

Moon, Michael. *Disseminating Whitman: Revision and Corporeality in Leaves of Grass.* Cambridge, Mass.: Harvard University Press, 1991.

Morris, Desmond. *The Naked Ape.* New York: Dell Publishing Co, Inc., 1969.

Murphy, Timothy F., Ph.D., ed. *Gay Ethics: Controversies in Outing, Civil Rights, and Sexual Science.* New York and London: The Haworth Press, 1994.

Murray, Stephen O. *American Gay.* Chicago: University of Chicago Press, 1996.

Nichols, Jack. "God's Gift to Atheism." *TWN* (*The Weekly News*), March 23, 1994.

———. *Men's Liberation: A New Definition of Masculinity.* New York: Penguin Books, 1975, 1980.

———. *Welcome to Fire Island: Visions of Cherry Grove and the Pines.* New York: St. Martin's Press, 1976.

Niebuhr, Gustav. "Two Bishops Sign Ad Backing Gay Rights: Clerics Join in Public Statement Responding to the Vatican's Stand." *Washington Post,* November 1, 1992, p. A–4.

Neider, John. *God, Sex & Your Child.* Nashville, Tenn.: Thomas Nelson, Inc., 1988.

Paine, Thomas. *Age of Reason.* Amherst, N.Y.: Prometheus Books, 1984.

Pear, Robert. "Rights Laws Offer Only Limited Help on AIDS, U.S. Rules." *New York Times,* June 23, 1986, Section A–1.

Pleck, Joseph, and Jack Sawyer, eds. *Men and Masculinity.* Englewood Cliffs, N.J.: Prentice-Hall, 1974.

Pomeroy, Wardell B., Clyde E. Martin, and Paul Gebhard. "Concepts of Normality and Abnormality in Sexual Behavior." In *Psychosexual Development in Health and Disease.* New York: Grune and Stratton, 1949, pp. 11–32.

Ramsey Colloquium. "The Homosexual Movement." *First Things, A Monthly Journal of Religion and Public Life,* No. 41, March 1994.

Ray, Ricky. "Ricky Ray 15, Dies: Barred From School Because of AIDS." *Washington Post,* December 14, 1992, Obituaries, p. D–8.

Raymond, Janice G. *The Transsexual Empire: The Making of the She-Male.* Boston: Beacon Press, 1979.

Rechy, John. *The Sexual Outlaw: A Documentary.* New York: Grove Weidenfeld/ Evergreen, 1989.

Reich, Wilhelm. *The Mass Psychology of Fascism,* trans. Theodore Wolfe. New York: Orgone Institute, 1946.

Reynolds, David S. *Walt Whitman's America: A Cultural Biography.* New York: Alfred A. Knopf, 1995.

Richmond, Len and Noguera. *The New Gay Liberation Book.* Palo Alto: Ramparts Press, 1979.

Riva, Maria. *Dietrich.* New York: Alfred A. Knopf, 1993.

Roberts, Sam. *Who We Are: A Portrait of America.* New York: Times Books, 1993.

Rowbotham, Sheila, and Jeffrey Weeks. *Socialism and the New Life: The Personal and Sexual Politics of Edward Carpenter.* London: Pluto Press, 1977.

Rubin, Jerry, and Mimi Leonard. *The War between the Sheets: What's Happening with Men in Bed and What Women and Men Are Doing About It.* New York: Richard Marek Publishers, 1980.

Russell, Bertrand. *Why I Am Not a Christian and Other Essays on Religion and Related Subjects.* London: George Allen & Unwin, Ltd., 1957.

Russell, Ina, ed. *Jeb and Dash: A Diary of Gay Life, 1918–1945.* Winchester, Mass.: Faber & Faber, Inc., 1993.

Russell, Paul. *The Gay 100: A Ranking of the Most Influential Gay Men and Lesbians, Past and Present.* New York: Carol Publishing Group, 1995.

Rutledge, Leigh W. *The Gay Decades.* New York: Plume Books, 1992.

———. *Unnatural Quotations.* Boston: Alyson Publications, 1988.

Sadownick, Douglas. *Sex between Men: An Intimate History of the Sex Lives of Gay Men Postwar to Present.* San Francisco: HarperCollins, 1996.

Safire, William. "What Fathers Want." *New York Times,* June 16, 1994, section A, p. 27.

Sanders, Jonathan. *Another Fine Dress: Role-Play in the Films of Laurel and Hardy.* London: Cassell, 1995.

Scruggs, David. "Falwell Says Bakker Must Not Return." *Orlando Sentinel,* March 26, 1987.

Sears, Dr. James T. *Growing Up Gay in the South.* Binghamton, N.Y.: Haworth, 1991.

———, ed. "Bound By Diversity." *Empathy* 4, nos. 1/2 (1994).

Sherman, Allan. *The Rape of the Ape.* Chicago: The Playboy Press, 1973.

Shilts, Randy. *And the Band Played On: Politics, People and the AIDS Epidemic.* New York: St. Martin's Press, 1987.

Simpson, Mark. *Male Impersonators: Men Performing Masculinity.* New York: Routledge, 1994.

Slansky, Paul. *The Clothes Have No Emperor: A Chronicle of the American 80s.* New York: Simon and Schuster, 1989.

Smith, Frank. *Robert G. Ingersoll: A Life.* Amherst, N.Y.: Prometheus Books, 1990.

Stevens, Joann. "The Boy Whore World." *Washington Post,* October 7, 1980, p. 1.

Stewart, Barbara. "Being Born Again: Anita Bryant Resurrected, She's Starting Fresh." *Florida* magazine, *Orlando Sentinel,* February 21, 1988.

Streitmatter, Dr. Rodger. "Lesbian and Gay Press: Raising a Militant Voice in the 1960s." *American Journalism* 12, no. 2 (Spring 1995).

———. *Unspeakable: The Rise of the Gay and Lesbian Press in America.* Boston and London: Faber & Faber, 1995.

Sullivan, Sheila "Lou." "Toward Transvestite Liberation." Milwaukee: *GPU News,* February-March, 1974.

Teal, Donn. *The Gay Militants: How Gay Liberation Began in America, 1969–1971.* New York: Stein and Day, 1971; first paperback edition, New York: St. Martin's Press, 1995.

Teller, Walter, ed. *Walt Whitman's Camden Conversations.* New Brunswick, N.J.: Rutger's University Press, 1973.

Thomas, Mike. "Are Gay Rights a Civil Right?" *Florida* magazine, *Orlando Sentinel,* July 18, 1993.

√ Thompson, Mark. *Gay Soul: Finding The Heart of Gay Spirit and Nature.* San Francisco: HarperCollins, 1995.

√ ———, ed. *Gay Spirit: Myth and Meaning.* New York: St. Martin's Press, 1987.

———. *Long Road to Freedom: The Advocate History of the Gay and Lesbian Movement.* New York: St. Martin's Press, 1994.

Tobin, Kay, and Randy Wicker. *The Gay Crusaders: In-Depth Interviews with 15 Homosexuals—Men and Women Who Are Shaping America's Newest Sexual Revolution.* New York: Paperback Library, 1971.

Truscott, Lucian, IV. "Gay Power Comes to Sheridan Square." *Village Voice,* July 3, 1969, p. 1.

Twain, Mark (Samuel Langhorne Clemens). "The Damned Human

Race." In *The Great Thoughts,* ed. George Seldes. New York: Ballatine Books, 1985, p. 83.

Ulrichs, Karl Heinrich. *The Riddle of Man-Manly Love,* trans. Michael A. Lombardi-Nash, foreword by Vern L. Bullough. Amherst: N.Y.: Prometheus Books, 1994.

✓ Vaid, Urvashi. *Virtual Equality: The Mainstreaming of Gay and Lesbian Liberation.* New York: Anchor Books, 1995.

Vidal, Gore. *Live from Golgotha.* New York: Random House, 1992.

———. *Messiah.* New York: Ballantine Books, 1984.

Warren, George. *The Dark Side of Conservatism: A Searing Indictment of the Conservative Movement.* Salt Lake City: Northwest Publishing, Inc., 1994.

Watts, Alan. *In My Own Way.* New York: Vintage Books, 1973.

Weinberg, George, Ph.D. *The Heart of Psychotherapy.* New York: St. Martin's Press, 1984.

———. *Invisible Masters.* New York: Plume/Penguin, 1995.

———. *Nearer to the Heart's Desire: Tales of Psychotherapy.* New York: Grove Press, 1992.

———. *The Pliant Animal: Understanding the Greatest Human Asset.* New York: St. Martin's Press, 1981.

———. *Self-Creation.* New York: Avon Books, 1978.

———. *Society and the Healthy Homosexual.* New York: St. Martin's Press, 1972.

———. *The Taboo Scarf and Other Tales of Therapy.* New York: Ballantine Books, 1990.

Weinberg, George, and Dianne Rowe. *Will Power.* New York: St. Martin's Press, 1996.

Wells, Paul O'M. *Project Lambda.* Port Washington, N.Y.: Ashley Books, Inc., 1979.

Weltge, Ralph W., ed. *The Same Sex: An Appraisal of Homosexuality.* Philadelphia and Boston: Pilgrim Press, 1969.

Wesley, Frank and Claire. *Sex-Role Psychology.* New York: Human Sciences Press, 1977.

✓ White, Mel. *Stranger at the Gate: To Be Gay and Christian in America.* New York: Simon and Schuster, 1994.

Whitman, Walt. "Democratic Vistas." In *Whitman Poetry and Prose,* texts selected by Justin Kaplan. New York: Literary Classics of the United States, 1982.

———. *Leaves of Grass.* Amherst, N.Y.: Prometheus Books, 1995.

———. *Leaves of Grass: "The Deathbed" Edition.* New York: The Modern Library, Random House, 1921.

Williams, Tennessee. *Collected Stories.* New York: Ballantine Books, 1986.

Woods, Gregory. *Articulate Flesh: Male Homo-Eroticism and Modern Poetry.* New Haven and London: Yale University Press, 1987.

Woog, Dan. *School's Out: The Impact of Gay and Lesbian Issues on America's Schools.* Boston: Alyson Publications, 1995.

Yang, John E. "House Bill to Save Gay Marriages Has Stormy Start." *Washington Post,* June 13, 1996, p. A–8.

Young, Ian. *The Stonewall Experiment: A Gay Psychohistory.* London: Cassell, 1995.

Zweig, Paul. *Walt Whitman: The Making of the Poet.* New York: Basic Books, Inc., 1984.

Index